Sensory Stories to Support Additional Needs

Other books published by Joanna Grace

Sharing Sensory Stories and Conversations with People with Dementia
A Practical Guide
Joanna Grace
ISBN 978 1 78592 409 5
eISBN 978 1 78450 769 5

of related interest

Sensory Solutions in the Classroom
The Teacher's Guide to Fidgeting, Inattention and Restlessness
Monique Thoonsen and Carmen Lamp
Illustrated by Ruud Bijman
Foreword by Winnie Dunn
ISBN 978 1 78592 697 6
eISBN 978 1 78592 698 3

Practical Sensory Programmes
For Students with Autism Spectrum Disorder and Other Special Needs
Sue Larkey
ISBN 978 1 84310 479 7
eISBN 978 1 84642 567 7

Multisensory Rooms and Environments
Controlled Sensory Experiences for People with Profound and Multiple Disabilities
Susan Fowler
Foreword by Paul Pagliano
ISBN 978 1 84310 462 9
eISBN 978 1 84642 809 8

Using Intensive Interaction and Sensory Integration
A Handbook for Those Who Support People with Severe Autistic Spectrum Disorder
Phoebe Caldwell with Jane Horwood
ISBN 978 1 84310 626 5
eISBN 978 1 84642 807 4

SENSORY STORIES TO SUPPORT ADDITIONAL NEEDS

Making Narratives Accessible Through the Senses

Joanna Grace

Forewords by Flo Longhorn and Martyn Sibley

Jessica Kingsley Publishers
London and Philadelphia

First edition published in 2014
This edition published in Great Britain in 2023 by Jessica Kingsley Publishers
An imprint of Hodder & Stoughton Ltd
An Hachette Company

I

A CIP catalogue record for this title is available from the
British Library and the Library of Congress

ISBN 978 1 83997 147 1
eISBN 978 1 83997 148 8

Printed and bound in Great Britain by CPI Group Ltd

Jessica Kingsley Publishers' policy is to use papers that are natural,
renewable and recyclable products and made from wood grown in
sustainable forests. The logging and manufacturing processes are expected
to conform to the environmental regulations of the country of origin.

Jessica Kingsley Publishers
Carmelite House
50 Victoria Embankment
London EC4Y 0DZ

www.jkp.com

This book is dedicated to the backers of the Sensory Story Project.

The ripples have spread further than we could ever have imagined.

Thank you!

Identity-first language is used in regards to autistic people in this book out of respect for, and in solidarity with, the autistic community who prefer it.

Contents

Foreword by Flo Longhorn. 9

Foreword by Martyn Sibley 11

Introduction 13

About This Book 15

PART I: BACKGROUND   17

1. The Importance of Sensory Stimulation. 19

2. The Significance of Narrative 28

PART II: SHARING SENSORY STORIES   37

3. How to Share a Sensory Story. 39

4. Sensory Stories for All 47

5. Sensory Processing Differences 51

6. Using Sensory Stories... 59

PART III: USING SENSORY STORIES AS A BASIS FOR ENGAGING AND INTERACTIVE SESSIONS   67

7. Supporting Learning and Development 69

8. Structuring Sessions to Challenge and Include a Range of People. . 71

9. A Nifty Assessment Tool 76

PART IV: THE SENSORY STORIES AND ASSOCIATED ACTIVITIES 79

10. About the Sensory Stories and Associated Activities. 81

PART V: GUEST STORIES 153

References 194

Further Reading 197

Index 199

Foreword

Flo Longhorn

This book tells a sensory story. It is for the seeker of sensory knowledge, who is looking for substantial ideas with which to plunge into new worlds of sensory storytelling. Each chapter offers a wealth of ideas and knowledge, including themes and ideas that could be placed at the core of a curriculum for special people.

I met the author, Jo Grace, when I recently funded part of her online 'Kickstarter Project' based on sensory stories, from which she launched her mission to write this book. It is a substantial book, which pulls together many different sensory strands, weaving them into a rich tapestry of sensory story creations. It also offers a sensory approach, reflected in the relevant anecdotal stories, notes and ideas of the writer included in each chapter.

Sensory stories for very special children and young people have developed over the last few years to become significant creative factors in their education and learning. This has evolved from the work of various 'hands-on' writers such as Keith Park, Melanie Nind, Pete Wells, Nicola Grove, Sheree Vickers and Andrea Muir to name a few, as well as the charity Bag Books. It has also been taken up in major dramas, reflected in theatre production groups such as Bamboozle, Oily Cart and Head2Head.

They all delight in pushing special people from concrete sensory stimulation into spontaneous and creative communications and fun. Jo's book joins this elite group.

When we dip into this book there are various significant strands, on a variety of different levels, to follow and explore:

- Sensory stimulation and learning dominates every life, from cradle to grave, without exception. For special people, it is the same but sensory stimulation should be a dominating and exciting feature of daily life and living.

- Sensory stories offer a powerful voice of communication. The participants can have a strong voice, either active or passive, so long as the reader listens and positively reacts to their voice.

- 'Including everyone' is a fundamental human belief, and sensory storytelling has no barriers.

- Sensory stories, ideas and resources usually have a base of concrete materials. These carefully selected sensory items arouse curiosity and exploration during the storytelling. Jo emphasizes that these materials should cost little or can be begged or borrowed. There is no need for expensive purchases. There is a need for imagination and forays into charity shops seeking them!

- On a research level, there is strong strand linking Jo's ideas to academic evidence within the book, gathered from significant educational research, writing and events.

I trust this book will reach and touch many readers, inspiring them to use sensory stories as a key to unlocking excitement, fun and enjoyment for every listener.

Flo Longhorn, author and principal consultant in special education

Foreword

Martyn Sibley

I've had my disability since birth. Spinal muscular atrophy is a genetic condition. Day to day it means I need a power wheelchair to sit up and move around. I have personal care assistants to support my independence. However, as long as I look after myself and maintain my independence, I'm only 'disabled' by societal barriers.

This may sound strange. Surely I'm disabled by this rare medical condition? But when you look at the social model of disability, it makes so much sense! For example, when I go to a café, if the building has steps, I'm disabled. If there's a ramp or is generally wheelchair accessible, I'm just Martyn. Another valued customer. If the customer service person on the till is scared or uncomfortable dealing with someone in a wheelchair, I'm disabled. But if they ask appropriate questions and assist me where helpful, I'm just Martyn. Another valued customer. Lastly if there is a procedure like not bringing food to a customers' table, I'm disabled. But if they are empowered to break the company-made rules for common sense and inclusion, I'm just Martyn. Another valued customer.

Some people think the job is done when disabled people have ramp access to buildings and toilets suitable to meet their needs, but not Joanna. Joanna wants access for everyone to everything, and that everything includes cultural experiences such as sharing in stories. In this book, Joanna explores the richness stories bring to our lives and uncovers for the reader how stories infiltrate every aspect of our lives, underpinning our friendships, defining our identities, guiding our decisions.

Joanna does not view some people as 'too disabled' to warrant access to sharing in stories, nor even, as the final story in this book stands in testimony to, 'too disabled' to be the author of stories shared. Through her use of sensory stimulation to convey meaning, Joanna weaves stories that are accessible to all. Stories you can touch, smell, move, taste, hear and see. Her guidance elucidates to the reader ways of sharing these stories that increase their impact. A person reading this book learns not just how to tell a story, but how to share a story that will resonate through someone's life, awakening their cultural sensitivities and empowering them as communicators with stories to share.

In the sensational landscape of a sensory story, everyone can meet as equals.

Martyn Sibley, Co-founder of Purple Goat and author of Everything is Possible

Introduction

WHAT IS A SENSORY STORY?

A sensory story is a story told using a combination of words and sensory experiences. The words and the experiences are of equal value when conveying the narrative. We know that sensory experiences are important and carry meaning: our instinctive interactions with infants are often in the form of sensory exchanges, and old adages such as 'a picture speaks a thousand words' and 'actions speak louder than words' testify to our knowledge that sensory stimuli convey meaning. Modern research, which will be discussed within this book, continues to provide further insight into the value of sharing stories in a sensory way.

Sensory stories were originally developed for people with profound and multiple learning disabilities by people such as Chris Fuller, Keith Park and Nicola Grove and organizations such as Bag Books and PAMIS (Full 1999a & b; Fuller in Grove 2012; Grove 2012; Grove and Park 1996, 2001; Young and Lambe 2011). They are a simple, engaging, fun resource, which can be used with people of all abilities. Part II of this book will give you ideas for how to use sensory stories to support people who face different challenges.

HOW I DISCOVERED SENSORY STORIES

I began my teaching career at a school for people with what was then termed 'severe and profound special educational needs and disabilities'. My class had a wide range of abilities and included a child with profound and multiple learning disabilities.

In addition to teaching my class, I was also expected to teach once a week in the class dedicated to people who had profound and multiple learning disabilities.

I had a lot to learn!

I was keen to do well and enthusiastically prepared lessons at the weekends and during school holidays that I hoped would work, but after delivering these lessons I was always left with a sense of having let down those people with profound and multiple learning disabilities. My teaching assistants were great and made sure everyone was involved in whatever task I had set, but I could read their faces and see they were thinking, 'Are you sure this is a good idea?' I was out of my depth. I was failing to communicate with all my students equally, and then another teacher in the school suggested I try a sensory story.

Sensory stories enabled me to teach my whole class; more than that, sharing sensory stories with the children with profound and multiple learning disabilities felt meaningful and I could clearly see that they were responding. By using sensory stories I was able to facilitate learning at a level appropriate to all people, including those with profound and multiple learning disabilities.

I was the biggest sensory story convert there has ever been. Sensory stories filled my teaching, touching everything from literacy to science, drama to physical education. I had a sensory story for every corner of the curriculum!

Since leaving the classroom, I have had the opportunity to read the research underpinning sensory learning. I was reassured to find many of the things that I had stumbled on while teaching were backed up by the research in the field. I wanted sensory stories to be available to everyone, not just to people time-rich enough to spend weeks puzzling over what would make a particular noise, or people with deep enough pockets to be able to afford pre-resourced stories. I also wanted to make sure that there were stories available for adults.

In 2013, I launched The Sensory Story Project, which aimed to create five resource-yourself affordable sensory stories. Thanks to numerous backers, The Sensory Story Project was a success: the stories were created, and the sale of those stories funded the writing of more stories. Today, the library of stories published by The Sensory Story Project continues to grow and collect new authors along the way, including authors who themselves have profound and multiple learning disabilities. This book is one of many wonderful things that have happened as a result of that project. You can find out more about The Sensory Story Project (and the sensory projects that followed on from it) at www.thesensoryprojects.co.uk.

About This Book

The following chapters introduce the importance of sensory stimulation and the significance of narrative, exploring the role that narrative has to play in inclusion. We look at the benefits gained from combining sensory stimulation and narrative together. Along the way, we also look at the senses we have (our famous five, plus two extra), what makes for strong sensory stimuli, and how it is possible for a short text to convey a whole story.

Part II of this book focuses on how sensory stories can be used in particular ways to support people who experience barriers to access when it comes to engaging in stories and communication.

Part III has practical suggestions for how to use sensory stories as a foundation for interactive and engaging sessions, and how to tell when to start telling a new story.

Part IV of this book contains five sensory stories together with activity suggestions to further engage with the stories and build on people's abilities.

Part V contains stories by some amazing guest authors, including a story authored by people with profound and multiple learning disabilities who, in the time since the first edition of this book was published, have moved from being consumers of this art form to creators of it!

More information can be found on my website www.thesensoryprojects.co.uk.

I hope you will find this book an enjoyable, easy and useful read.

I am easily contactable through social media and love to hear about your sensory adventures. Have fun creating and sharing sensory stories together.

PART I

BACKGROUND

Chapter 1

THE IMPORTANCE OF SENSORY STIMULATION

Sensory stimulation is central to our cognitive development (Ayer 1998). It is not just useful or an added extra; it is necessary. When a child is born, it is the information received through its senses that wires its brain (Bruner 1959; Gabbard and Rodrigues 2007; Piaget 1952).

One easy way to think about early cognitive development is to consider the brain as a densely overgrown forest. When we have a sensory experience, it sends an electronic pulse through our mind, creating a neural trace. If this experience is repeated, the trace becomes a pathway. Think of the experience as a person walking through it; they wouldn't make much of an impact, but as they walk more, the pathway would become well worn.

Experiences from different senses form different pathways through the forest. At a point where two pathways intersect, coordination develops between our senses. When sight coordinates with touch (or proprioception) we develop hand-eye coordination. The development of hand-eye coordination is not possible without first experiencing a wide range of sensory stimuli. Many important developmental milestones follow from the development of hand-eye coordination.

Sensory stimulation is not only necessary for brain development, it is also necessary for the maintenance of our faculties (Bruner 1959). In the forest of the mind, if a well-trodden path were no longer walked it would grow over and become lost. Most of us lead lives in which we will never experience the sort of sensory deprivation that could cause the loss of our abilities. However, some people may have to live in environments that are low in sensory stimulation; other people may purposefully avoid sensory stimulation (Chapter 5 on sensory processing differences will explain more about why they may do this); other people's access to sensory stimulation may be limited by their physical abilities.

Early on in my career, I attended a Richard Hirstwood training session. Training aimed specifically at people who worked in special schools was very hard to come by, particularly in rural Cornwall, so I was very excited to find such a relevant course. Richard told a story that serves as a very stark illustration of the 'use it or lose it' aspect of our sensory abilities. At the time, I did not see it as a story so much as a test. Here is what happened.

It was the start of the day. I was in a room full of people who did similar work to me. Many had been in their roles for 20–30 years; I had been in my job for just two years. I was very nervous. Richard welcomed us and explained that the first thing he wanted to do was tell us about a man he had worked with and we were then to diagnose this gentleman. I was alarmed; I thought that Richard was testing us to see how knowledgeable we were before he continued with the day. I knew I didn't stand a chance at guessing the condition of someone I hadn't met.

The man Richard described had a hunched-over body position and limited movement of his limbs. He could walk, but not very far. He did not respond to visual or auditory stimuli and did not speak. His eyes, ears and vocal cords had been tested, and as far as the medical profession knew there was nothing physically wrong with them. I had no idea what condition was being described, but a few more senior members of the group put their hands up and guessed at rare conditions that I had never heard of. They were wrong. That the experts got it wrong gave other people the courage to venture answers. The guesses got progressively vaguer, 'Was it some type of this, or a sort of that?' people wondered aloud. Richard kept up a steady stream of 'no' in response.

Finally, Richard told us what had happened to the man. When he was 17 he had broken up with his girlfriend and as a consequence had become very depressed, not getting out of bed in the morning and crying constantly. His parents were so distressed by his state that they had him committed to a local asylum. There he was put into bed by staff each evening, and in the morning he was got up and sat in a chair beside the bed. Each day this was repeated: bed in the evening; chair in the morning. Bed-chair, bed-chair, bed-chair. This cycle was maintained for 15 years.

The man's body was the shape of the chair he had sat in for those 15 years. It was not that he had become blind but that he had become personally disconnected from his sense of sight. He had no interest in seeing anymore: he'd seen the same view for 15 years. The same applied to his hearing. His needs had always been met. He'd had no reason to communicate. Without reason or cause to use his senses or his abilities, he had gradually shut down and withdrawn entirely into an inward world.

We are all so accustomed to living sensorially rich lives that it is easy for us to overlook the need for sensory stimulation – to think of it as a fun activity and nothing more. Sensory stimulation is vital for our development and essential for a happy life.

SENSORY STIMULATION AND CHILDREN WITH PHYSICAL OR SENSORY DIFFERENCES

We instinctively know the importance of sensory stimulation to the developing child; we dangle bright objects above babies, make silly noises, give them tactile toys to grab and chew. All of these things are great for promoting their cognitive development, but we should not underestimate just how much sensory stimulation a developing child accesses independently.

Imagine a typically developing child lying in their cot: the child hears a noise and turns their head to see what made the sound; the child spots a splodge of colour and reaches out with a hand to investigate what it might be. A typically developing child engages pretty much constantly in this sort of activity. All of these small investigations help to develop neural pathways in their mind.

Now imagine a child with profound physical disabilities lying in a cot; the child hears a noise but cannot turn their head; the child sees a shape but cannot reach out to investigate further. They do not have as much access to stimulation as their able-bodied peers.

Researchers investigating different aspects of provision for people with disabilities all comment on the diagnostic overshadowing which can occur (e.g. Hayes *et al.* 2011). It is very easy for people to believe that the cognitive delay observed in children with profound and multiple learning disabilities is a direct result of their disability, and not question whether it is a consequence of their not having had as much stimulation as typically developing peers. Yet if we look to the research that talks about early cognitive development and the importance of sensory stimulation, we find a wealth of researchers talking about how important the environment and the stimulation within it is to development (e.g. Glenn 1987; Gray and Chasey 2006; Hayes *et al.* 2011; Lacey 2009; Longhorn 1988; Vlaskamp *et al.* 2007; Ware 2003, cited in Gray and Chasey 2006). Ayer (1998, p.89) stressed the importance of sensory stimulation to development by saying, with reference to hand-eye coordination: 'The child with profound and multiple learning disabilities, combined with sensory and physical impairments, requires a sensory curriculum in order to bring them to this important stage of intellectual and motor development.'

The child who is unable to access sensory stimulation on their own begins their development on the back foot. It is very important that carers seek to provide people with profound disabilities with a wide range of sensory experiences. Sensory stories are one way of offering such stimulation.

The inability to access sensory stimulation independently not only affects a child's neurological development but also their attitude towards learning and engagement with life. Researchers found that some of the perceived passivity observed in people with profound and multiple learning disabilities was not solely down to their disabilities, as had previously been assumed, but was a form of learned helplessness. Hayes *et al.* (2011) report people with profound intellectual disabilities as suffering with low mood, making them less likely to engage in activities. They also found low mood could be the cause of negative behaviours displayed by autistic people, and speculated that antidepressants could be a more effective treatment than the currently prescribed tranquilizers.

Reflecting on the newborn child in their cot, it is easy to see how this could occur. The child lies in their cot, hears a sound and wants to turn their head to see what made the noise, but cannot. The child sees a shape and wants to reach out for it, but cannot. The child is interested in the world, curious about it, keen to engage with it, but learns over and over again that it is out of reach. It is natural that they will eventually give up trying to find out about it. Children unable to access the world around them can turn inwards for stimulation, and become disengaged with the world. This limits their ability to learn and their desire to communicate. In extreme cases people will self-harm in order to get the stimulation they desire.[1]

Sensory stories are one way of providing people with a range of sensory experiences.

OUR SENSES – THE FAMOUS FIVE, PLUS TWO

We have five famous senses and a few others that not everyone has heard about. The five famous ones are touch, taste, hearing, smell and sight. As our understanding of the sensory world develops, the way we count our sensory systems grows increasingly more intricate. In the first edition of this book, the count was up to 18, but you can now find me saying 33 (a number I picked up from exploring conversations shared by Draper (2019), Fairhurst (2014) and

---

[1]   It is important to note that self-harm in people with profound and multiple learning disabilities can also indicate that they are feeling pain.

Macpherson (2011) and which I first read about in an article about neuron sets – it is an evolving conversation!).

But for the purpose of this book, I am adding just two more to the famous five: our vestibular sense and our proprioceptive sense. We use these senses to help us to understand where our body is and what is happening to us.

Your vestibular sense relates to balance and movement. Picture yourself in a completely closed-in, sound-insulated lift. You know when it starts to move. You have not used your sense of sight, because it is completely closed in. You did not use your ability to hear, because it is sound insulated so you are not able to hear the motor start. You did not use taste or smell, and the only touch you experienced was your feet against the floor. It is your vestibular sense that tells you that the lift is moving.

Your proprioceptive sense tells you where your body is in space. Try this experiment: put a cup on a table then turn around and reach behind you with your hand to pick up the cup. My bet is that you are able to do this with relative ease. I expect that you reached straight for the cup – you did not look, you certainly could not hear where the cup was, nor did you sniff or taste your way there. You might have felt your way along the edge of the table, but I doubt it; I expect you were able to reach straight for the cup. You were able to reach for the cup without looking because you knew where it was and you knew where your body was in space; that is your proprioceptive sense in action.

As with your other senses, your vestibular and proprioceptive senses can be impaired. A person may have stronger or weaker proprioception. People with low proprioceptive sense will seek to discover where their body is through their other senses; this counters the unnerving sensation of not quite knowing where their body is. Someone who experiences difficulties with their proprioception may well fidget a lot because this will give them feedback through their sense of touch as to where they are. Similarly, tipping and spinning can be ways of amplifying the information received by the brain from the vestibular sense.

Teachers and parents may view a child who is engaged in something like fidgeting or spinning as being distracted from their learning. I am not saying every child who tips their chair or fidgets is experiencing sensory differences, but I can say that it is possible that these sorts of behaviours help, rather than hinder, a child's concentration.

A person in a state of anxiety is not in an optimal state for learning. Fear activates our primitive fight or flight response, which actually bypasses the part of the brain responsible for learning. A frightened person will not learn and cannot learn, they will not be able to engage with an activity, with life.

A person who feels anxious because they are unsure where their body is will look to soothe that anxiety in some way. If they are able to soothe their anxiety then they will be in a state ready to learn. As people who care, it is our job to find ways to provide for people's needs in a manner that suits their environment; for example, a person who seeks feedback about where their body is by tipping their chair can be given an elastic physio band (or a pair of tights) to wrap around the legs of their chair; they can then press against this band with their feet and get the feedback they need without distracting other people. Other people respond well to being given small toys to fiddle with while they listen, or feel less anxious when wearing compression clothing.

WHAT MAKES FOR STRONG SENSORY STIMULI?

Sensory stories are told using words and sensory stimuli. Unlike a picture book, the stimuli are not merely an accompaniment to the words; they are as much the story as the words are, so just as we choose the right words for a story, we should also choose the right stimuli for a story.

When picking sensory stimuli to tell a story I think about two things: how great an experience does the stimulus give, and how connected is the stimulus to the story I want to tell? To tell a good sensory story, you need to get both these things right. It is no good having a great set of sensory stimuli that have nothing whatsoever to do with the narrative, or bending the narrative to fit the stimuli you happen to have, or having a great story that is told through a weak selection of sensory stimuli.

A strong sensory stimulus is one that wholly engages a sense, or one that demands attention from a sense. Children's books are often illustrated with pictures. A picture is not a strong visual experience by itself. To be interested in a picture you need prior knowledge about what a picture does, an understanding that pictures convey information and represent life, and you need to be interested in what might be in that picture. Without this understanding, a picture is just a selection of coloured blobs in a particular location.

Imagine a teacher reading a picture book in front of the class. The teacher presents the children with a page of colours and lines. On the classroom walls behind the teacher are colourful posters, to the side are the children's coats and bags of different colours and textures, and on the tables are colourful pencil tins. The children have no reason to look at the picture in terms of its visual features alone.

A strong visual experience could be something that impacts your whole vision. It need not be complicated – looking through a sheet of coloured cellophane changes *everything* you see; it is a big visual experience. The absence of light – for example, experiencing total darkness from a blindfold – is another big visual experience. Things with high contrast – for example, bright lights against dark backgrounds or an indoor sparkler – will also naturally draw the eye and be strong visual experiences. Moving items may also draw the eye more strongly than static objects, as the sensors in our eyes that pick up on movement are different from those that record colour and shape. Some people may find it easier to perceive a moving object than a static one, for other people the opposite will be true.

Once you start to question experiences in this way it becomes easier to discern what makes a strong sensory stimulus. A strong touch experience does not have to be experienced with the whole body, although a whole-body experience, such as being submerged in water, would certainly be very strong, if a little difficult to facilitate within the context of a story. I encourage you to try touch experiences out and see what makes you pay attention. Think about where a touch experience happens; we do not have to touch with our hands. The skin on our forearms or the soles of our feet is very sensitive – touch experiences are stronger if delivered to sensitive locations on the body. How we experience touch can also affect its relevance to a story. Consider a story about a trip to the beach; would feeling sand between your toes be a more pertinent experience than sand on your hands? A favourite touch experience of mine is to create a teardrop using a small pipette or a drinking straw to drop a tear onto a person's cheek exactly where a tear that had been cried would fall. That feeling of a tear trickling down your face is a very particular feeling. The skin on your cheek by your nose is very sensitive. It is an experience you notice and pay attention to, which makes it a strong experience in itself. If used to tell the part of a story where someone is crying, the connection to that part of the story is a strong experience, because that *is* what a tear feels like as it runs down your face.

It is good to be creative when thinking about touch experiences. I have seen cuddly toys used as touch experiences – does a toy lion really offer a similar touch experience to a wild lion? I have seen swatches of fabric used to represent a character's clothing, and I am left wondering whether this was an important part of the story. To be interested in what the character's clothes feel like, first I have to know there is a character, and to understand anything about that character from touching their clothes, I have to understand the significance of silks, lace and gold embellishments and so on. It depends on the fabric, but many will not make for strong touch experiences because we so commonly touch fabric in daily life. I expect today you woke up touching the fabric of a sheet and blanket and maybe your nightwear; you then got up and touched a range of other fabrics as you put on your socks, underwear and clothes. You may also have touched tea towels, bandages, nappies, coats, scarves, cuddly toys, curtains, bags and so on throughout the day. My guess is that if your hand brushed against a piece of fabric you would not stop to see what it was; however, if you put your hand in something sticky, you would stop and look, want to know what it was and even shriek and pull away. A good touch experience will grab your attention; a really great one will not only grab your attention but also be relevant to the story and make you want to explore it further.

What makes for a strong sensory experience is personal to each person. In the above paragraph, I gave an account of a life where fabric was commonplace, but suppose I was a child growing up in poverty – in a slum, without clothing. I am more likely to have touched a plastic bag than a piece of velvet. To that child, touching a swatch of satin or fur fabric would be a big experience. When choosing sensory stimuli for a story we need to be aware of our own sensory experiences of the world and also of the experiences of the person with whom we intend to share the story. In my collaboration with speech and language therapists Rebecca Leighton and Coralie Oddy, who work with people with dementia, we explored what would constitute strong sensory experiences that relate to their youth: the whistle of a kettle on the hob, an air raid siren, mint humbugs, sherbet dips, carbolic soap and so on. Sensory experiences are personal to each person and influenced by their abilities, experiences, preferences, life and the times they live in. (To learn more about this work read my book, *Sharing Sensory Stories and Conversations with People with Dementia* (2018a), and the publication I wrote with Rebecca Leighton and Coralie Oddy, 'Using sensory stories with individuals with dementia' which was published in both the UK and Australian editions of the *Journal of Dementia Care* (2016)).

Sound and taste experiences are usually easier to discern in storytelling, as they tend to be the items from the story. For example, in a story where someone eats a sandwich, you can eat a sandwich. In a story where a drummer plays, you can play a drum. Sound and taste are also two senses we typically pay more attention to. We know what we like and do not like to eat; we can become passionate about flavours, returning to a restaurant for a particular sauce or begging a friend for a particular recipe. We have favourite songs and bands, and we know how our emotions are swayed by different sorts of music. Through our experience of sound and taste, we enrich our lives; a pleasurable taste or sound experience is a luxury to us – a treat, something we value – so most people have a pretty good idea of what makes for strong sensory experiences in regards to these senses.

Taste does not have to be an experience only for those who are able to chew and swallow. Many people with profound and multiple learning disabilities are tube fed and cannot take food orally. A taste experience can still be provided by touching a flavour to the tongue. Pineapple juice is said to stimulate more taste buds than any other flavour; a drip of it on the tongue could be a rich taste experience. Some experiences lie on the boundary between taste and touch; consider an ice cube held against the lips or a metal spoon in the mouth – both could be thought of as taste experiences. Today you can buy many different flavours of lip balm, which can also be used as taste experiences where actual food is not appropriate. Make sure to be fully aware of a person's medical history before sharing taste experiences with someone who does not eat food; saliva production can be safe for some people, dangerous to others.

Smell is generally a pretty overlooked sense, yet people in old age often remark on how certain aromas take them back to a particular time in their life. For me, the smell of Stickle Bricks will always take me back to my first primary school classroom. If I asked you what you smelt yesterday you would probably struggle to remember unless something significant had happened to you. Thinking about what smells you remember can provide clues as to what would make a great smell experience. Of course, particularly pungent smells come high up the list – if you stepped in dog poo yesterday you would remember the smell but that sort of smell can be difficult to share safely with someone in the context of a story, so keep thinking. Perhaps you smelt a loved one's perfume? Perhaps it was the smell of something fantastic cooking?

Thinking about what would make a good stimulus for the proprioceptive or vestibular sense can be tricky, as our awareness of these senses is new. Movement can be used to address both of these senses, and touch experiences often combine to form proprioceptive experiences as well. As with all of the senses, by simply paying attention to our own experiences in everyday life we develop our insight into what makes a strong experience in the context of a sensory story.

For more insight into the richness of sensory experience and how to determine what would make a truly engaging sensory experience for someone who has profound and multiple learning disabilities look up my book *Sensory-Being for Sensory Beings* (Grace 2018b).

Chapter 2

THE SIGNIFICANCE
OF NARRATIVE

The word 'story' conjures up pictures in our mind of childhood storybooks and sweet tales told to young children to get them to sleep at night. Stories are not just relics of childhood; they permeate our lives and contribute to forming our identities. There are the stories we tell each other about what we did at the weekend, whether our team won or lost and what he or she said at work the other day. There are the stories we share from our history, culture or faith group. There are the stories we've been told about who we were when we were little. There are the stories we share in together through films, TV and books. Stories enrich all our lives.

The ability to form our experiences into a story helps us to hold on to and remember them. Stories help us to share our experiences and interest others in our lives. In sharing a story, we seek out and receive acknowledgement that our lives are interesting and of value to others. We interest others in us and draw others close to us, furnishing our lives with friendships, which are necessary for such social animals as ourselves.

Through listening to other people's stories, we learn things about life without having to experience them ourselves, just as stories with morals in them teach us right from wrong. Listening to other people's stories allows us to think about what we would have done in the situation they describe. Stories let us decide who we will be, and how to design our own identities. Many people will hold characters from stories up as heroes or models for their life, striving to emulate aspects of those characters in their own life.

The telling of a story, and sharing in that telling, is a bonding social event. This is true of all sorts of stories, from those read from the pulpits of churches, uniting the parishioners in a shared set of beliefs, to those told in pubs, on buses, or at home. Joining in with these stories, whether it is by saying 'Amen' or by laughing along at the appropriate points, is our way of saying, 'I am part of this', and 'I am with you in this life, we are not alone.' Not to be included or able to join in is to be isolated and alienated in the extreme.

Families will tell stories of events they all shared in: remember that Christmas when Grandma sat on the cat? These shared reminiscences and 'in' jokes bond us and form part of our identity. We are told stories about who we were when we were little – these shape our notion of self. We share in stories from our culture, history and time. Some sound more worthy than others, but all have their part to play; for example, when I was a teenager the TV series *Friends* was hugely popular. I know if I meet someone who is roughly my age and I quote a line from *Friends*, they are likely to know what I am on about. We will have something in common; we will feel a connection, just through sharing in a story. The person who cannot share in these common stories misses out on being able to form connections with others in this way.

I have a small personal insight into what it is like to be the one left out of these stories. When I was a child I lived on a boat. It is my childhood depicted in the sensory story *Ernest and I* (Grace 2018c). I watched dolphins leaping over the boat's bow waves and played on deserted beaches. It was a wonderful childhood. We settled on land around the time I started school. The boat did not have a TV and neither did our new house. I did not notice the absence of TV until I was in the playground. Gaggles of children would circle the playground inviting people to play games with them. I was invited to play Ewoks – I had no idea what an Ewok was, so I could not play. Other games offered were: She-Ra, The A-Team and Muppet Babies – all equally puzzling to me. The children wanted to include me but they could not because I did not share in those stories with them; when I tried to engage them in conversation about beaches and dolphins, they did not understand.

To be left out of stories is to be left out of a part of life. When we seek to include people who are differently abled in life, inclusion in stories should be a part of that, not only in sharing stories but also in the characters.

Gwendolen Benjamin contributed the narrative to *The Forest of Thorns* story which appears in Part V of this book. Here, Gwen talks in her own words about the links between stories and society:

Stories are in a constant dialogue with society. Each generation is shaped by the stories of those that came before, and then goes on to tell their own stories. Secondary socialization is the process by which we learn norms and values from the society in which we are raised. This includes the stories we read or are told. Any stories we create will be unavoidably influenced by our norms and values.

This can take an insidious form. The term 'The Smurfette Principle' was coined in 1991 by writer Katha Pollitt, who noted that, too often, a single female character is included in an ensemble cast, solely playing the role of the token girl. This reinforces the idea that male is the default gender and women take a secondary role. A similar effect can be seen in the ratio of white to non-white characters in Western media. A sole instance of this in a story may not cause a problem, but when we are exposed to the same idea over and over it can become normalized. As a writer, I try to be hyper aware of any messages my work may be conveying, because I am aware of the power they can have. While stories can be an immense power for good, they can also be damaging.

We can see how stories and society are entertained by looking at the way world events affect what stories are told. I am a huge nerd, so I love Star Trek. When the original series first aired in 1966 the Cold War was in full swing and this is reflected all over the stories. The most obvious example is the Federation's tense relationship with the major villains: the Klingon Empire. Mysterious, militarized and clearly dangerous opponents, the Klingons embody a stereotypical view of life behind the Iron Curtain. As the Cold War petered out and the franchise continued, their portrayal becomes more nuanced and sympathetic. Early in 2013, the film Star Trek Into Darkness was released. One of the driving events of the film is a terrorist attack and the reactions to it, reflecting life in a post-9/11 world.

Stories reacting to shared traumatic events are nothing new. Noah's Ark can be taken as an example: God floods the entire world, tasking Noah with rescuing animals so life may continue. Stories of a global flood can be found in many cultures, including one of the oldest surviving stories: the Epic of Gilgamesh. It is likely that these are a response to a large-scale flood, or a number of them, that really happened. Stories about such events serve as a record of them, but they are also a safe space to deal with them. Putting something in a fictional context can remove the real-life baggage that surrounds it, making it easier to re-examine.

Gwen is beginning to touch on what researchers have termed 'the storytelling space'. The space in which stories are told and shared has been found to have special properties. In the storytelling space, we are braver, we feel more confident and we are better able to cope with life's challenges. In the storytelling space, we are omniscient and unafraid, we understand things better than we do in real life and we can face things we fear. Jo Empson's book *Rabbityness* (2012) is a good example of the way this special space can be utilized. *Rabbityness* is a beautiful book in which one rabbit dies and the other rabbits mourn him by finding ways to remember him that make them happy. I have used this book many times to talk to children about how to respond to bereavement. Children who would not know how to talk about the death of their grandfather, pet or friend find in *Rabbityness* a way of telling me about what their loved one was like and quickly come up with things their loved one enjoyed doing. I can also recommend Sarah Helton's (2017) *A Special Kind of Grief*, and my own sensory story *When You Were Gone* (2016) as useful tools for supporting people with complex disabilities in their grief.

Sharing in stories makes our lives richer and bonds us together. To share stories with people in a way that is meaningful to them is to include them in life and to offer them the opportunity to benefit from all the wonderful things narrative has to offer us. Sharing sensory stories is one way of doing this.

WHY COMBINE SENSORY STIMULATION AND STORYTELLING?

Sensory storytelling provides both the opportunity to deliver richly stimulating sensory experiences to a person and to share a story with them. The story aspect adds a structure to the sensory stimulation, and this structure can be further reinforced by maintaining the consistency explained in Chapter 3 of this book. Having a clear structure means that experiences can be repeated. Repeating experiences increases their predictability to the person experiencing them, and this in turn increases feelings of security that the person will feel in relation to the experiences. Repetition is important for learning to occur. Presenting experiences in a structured way enables the development of memory and anticipation (Gray and Chasey 2006).

Sensory stimulation is valuable in and of itself; I am not advocating that all sensory activities should be structured. We should aim to present people with a range of activities, regardless of their abilities. When we consider the activities that take place in a typical school, or indeed in the course of a typical day for most people, some will be more structured than others. Some people flourish where there is structure and others flourish where activities are relatively free flowing. If we present only unstructured, or only structured activities to people, we limit their opportunities.

WHAT CAN YOU SAY IN TEN SENTENCES?

Sensory stories are usually pretty short. The stories in this book are all under ten phrases, and the content of each phrase is intentionally concise. Researcher Penny Lacey writing in *PMLD Link* (2006) said that sensory stories are literacy for people with profound and multiple learning disabilities.

Penny is highlighting that sensory stories are not a substitute for the real thing; they can be the real thing. Other researchers add weight to the value of sharing sensory stories with people with profound disabilities (Grace and Silva 2017; Lambe *et al.* 2014; Preece and Zhao 2015; Watson 2002; Young *et al.* 2011). Engaging in sensory storytelling is a valuable literacy activity for people with profound and multiple learning disabilities, not a substitute for literacy. Literature covers a rich and broad range of writings, from poetry to fairy tales, sci-fi to chic lit, historical fiction to literary fiction. I hope that one day sensory stories will span as broad a range.

It might seem improbable that different genres of writing could all be created within so few sentences, but it is possible.

As part of The Sensory Story Project, I worked with a physicist to create sensory story about the birth of stars in stellar nurseries. In seven sentences, we were able to explain all the essential facts involved in the formation of stars and convey them in a way that came together as an interesting and engaging narrative. We created a very concise piece of non-fiction. Another Sensory Story Project story, *Puddle*, is told in the form of a haiku; it is a piece of poetry. Within this book, you will find a wide range of stories from folklore to sci-fi. You will find stories suitable to story experiencers of all ages. Gwen's story is based on the traditional fairy tale of *Sleeping Beauty* and is written in the fantasy realism style, so that is another two genres ticked off the list. We are getting there, and we are not the only ones: PAMIS (Promoting A More Inclusive Society) is a Scottish charity that has created stories based around what are seen as sensitive topics, such as personal hygiene. Bag Books is a UK charity that creates resourced sensory stories that tell fun children's stories about trips out or magical adventures, and Pete Wells writes anarchic narratives that often involve joyously disgusting things like farts and snot. (You can listen to Pete discussing these on his sensory story podcast: https://sensorystoriespodcast.com and you will find a story from him appearing later on in this book!) More and more sensory storytellers pop up every day – hop onto social media for the latest! Since 2020, The Sensory Story Project has been publishing sensory stories by other authors.

You can read about some of the sensory story adventures I have been on since the dawning of The Sensory Story Project in the next section. But the adventures have not all been mine. It has been an absolute pleasure to witness over the past decade a continued expansion in the stories that are available to people with profound and multiple learning disabilities. I trust it is an expansion that will continue to blossom.

SENSORY STORY ADVENTURES

When I set up The Sensory Story Project I had dared to dream that I would write five stories. My chances of fulfilling that dream stood at around 16 per cent (that was the percentage of Kickstarter Projects at that time that reached their funding goals). It was fanciful. I wrote to the backers of the project that their contribution was like throwing a pebble in a pond, and that the ripples would spread. Never in my wildest dreams did I imagine they would spread this far.

Shortly after that initial Kickstarter campaign was successful I was invited to write the first edition of this book. As people bought the first five stories I was able to fund the writing of more. As I put my fingers to the keyboard today, the number of stories published by the project stands at 25, and around a dozen more stories have been published in collaboration with other organizations, including Exeter University, Simple Stuff Works and the Sensory Trust.

I am by nature a quiet introverted person. To give you an example: I attended a small primary school, where every child was expected to take a role in the school plays, even if it was just singing in the chorus line. Every child, except me. My teachers knew that to ask someone as shy as me to stand up on stage would be cruel, so roles were invented for me: I turned the pages for the piano teacher, I was in charge of hauling the curtains open and closed, I ran continuity backstage (a job which consisted solely of standing backstage and not making a noise). That is me. In creating The Sensory Story Project I imagined being an author. I had not anticipated that the publicity the project received and the publication of this book would result in me being asked to provide training to others, but of course it did.

I began my training career nervously in front of a room full of adult care workers in London. I was to tell them about sensory stories. I never did find the confidence I lacked as a child, but what I discovered in that room, and all the rooms since then, is that I was so excited to tell people about sensory stories that it didn't matter. I had confidence in those people that they would be kind to me; if I fumbled my words, they would not mind. Before the end of that year I was talking about sensory stories at the UK's biggest special educational needs conference, TES SEN, and in the years since I have presented on various platforms globally, and I am currently preparing a masterclass in sensory stories for the International Storytelling Festival in Singapore. My excitement about sensory stories has not waned yet.

From time to time, I feel wobbly. I am still at heart the child hiding backstage, keeping quiet. I enjoy the connection with people that social media affords, and I've found that the internet has some sort of magic within it, because whenever I've felt unsure a message will pop up from someone and remind me how privileged I am to get to do what I do. Every time someone shares their experience with me it is precious to me but some messages last in the memory more than others. I remember a message from a young woman who worked in an institution in another country; she explained that the people with profound disabilities were all housed in the basement and did not have access to activities. She wondered to me whether she might, on her own, be able to tell them sensory stories. In the years that followed we corresponded as she created and shared a range of sensory stories with these people, many of whom had spent their whole lives in those rooms. The photos she shared of them tasting things, touching things, give me enough reason to brave the next stage, the next microphone!

Another message came from a mother to a young boy with profound disabilities, 'Do you think I could read my son a story?' she asked. Their lives until that point had been all about his medical care needs, and she felt herself so disabled by all she had not been able to do for him that she doubted her ability to do something as simple as read a story to her child. With a few simple words of encouragement from me their sensory story adventures began and I still get little photographic glimpses into them. Other messages contained phrases that stick in the mind: 'My neighbour has a child; they do not bring him out the house.' 'He has been here for sixteen years and is completely unresponsive.' I spend my evenings writing back. People take my words and do life-changing things with them. I stand in awe of them. The words are like seeds, and those people are the most green-fingered of gardeners. I'm not sure I could do the same with them; I have the seeds, but not the bravery to go and knock on the neighbour's door as that messenger did, or stand up to the system within their setting that had denied those people a sensory curriculum, as the second messenger did. I get mocked for the time I spend on social media and if you judged me for what shows publicly I'm sure I look as self-absorbed as everyone ends up looking on social media, but the noise I make there reaches around the world, and the backstage bit is those messages, and they're worth all the judgement.

As well as publishing stories, delivering training and presentations and making a noise online, there have been some fabulous sensory story adventures in the past ten years. I have experienced sensory stories created by people who have attended my training or read my books. Among the most memorable have been the Black Honey Bee trail created at Heligan Gardens in Cornwall (which you can see here: https://tinyurl.com/y52wrcuw) and Frozen Light's amazing Isle of Brimsker (www.frozenlighttheatre.com/

previousshows/theisleofbrimsker). I have shared sensory stories with people with dementia, and you can read more about this in *Sharing Sensory Stories and Conversations with People with Dementia* (Grace 2018a) and see one such adventure here: https://tinyurl.com/wt8e3v77.

I have been employed to create sensory tours of some amazing places and spaces, most memorably the King's State Apartments at Kensington Palace and the London Transport Museum. At other times, I've worked with people to discover sensory stories. I remember a fantastic day with the Sensory Trust at King Edward Mine in Cornwall, hunting for sensory adventures and then discovering in their museum a near ready-made sensory story in the form of an old sign explaining the emergency procedure for fire! You can see the adventures here: https://tinyurl.com/42t62cpk. I have created sensory access stories, stories that explain the sensations of a novel experience, allowing people to prepare for that experience or have a little of that experience if the actual experience is inaccessible. As I write, I sit next to boxes full of the sensations of kayaking about to be posted out as part of a project with Exeter University and Sensing Nature – this year it is kayaking, last year it was the circus! You can watch a short film about the Circus Starr sensory access story here: www.circus-starr.org.uk/sensorystory.

Speaking at conferences means I get to meet some amazing organizations. At one event looking at how people with learning disabilities are supported into adulthood I met the founder of Parallel, Andrew Douglass. Through an odd chain of events involving Changing Places toilets and a total tech failure during my sensory story presentation, I ended up pondering aloud the idea for the Super Sensory. Parallel is a mass participation sporting event – think the Olympics but for everybody! The Super Sensory sees racers travel along a course of sensations, and every 100 meters a new sensory experience is presented. Racers can train for the race by exploring these sensations ahead of time. On the day, people for whom the limit of their physical ability is to look, touch, and smell, are cheered on with as much respect and enthusiasm as they push themselves to their limits as any Olympian is. Standing on the finish line of the Super Sensory – as has been my privilege as an Ambassador for Parallel – is one of the most exhilarating places on earth. (You can see a glimpse here: https://tinyurl.com/2r44s7p2 and here: https://tinyurl.com/ybe7rm2b and here: https://tinyurl.com/hb9s4f and here: https://tinyurl.com/2zas7s9a and here: https://tinyurl.com/h8b5pk45, the number of links is indicative of how exciting it is.)

Seeing people anticipate experiences in a sensory story remains one of the most thrilling aspects of sensory storytelling for me. (You can see an example here: https://tinyurl.com/89veza98.) Moments spent in the storytelling space shared with another human are some of the best moments in life. But perhaps most joyous of all since beginning the adventure of The Sensory Story Project, I have witnessed the experiencers of the stories become the authors of the stories, drawing a parallel with other art forms and with the creation of mainstream literature where you would expect to see in time the consumers become the creators. The days I have spent acting as a facilitator for groups of people with profound and multiple learning disabilities co-authoring their own sensory stories are easily some of the best days of my life, and I am looking forward to more of them! You can read about the co-authorings in *PMLD Link* (Grace and Robinson 2017) and in SEN Leader (Grace 2019). Being a part of them was like being given permission to walk around inside someone else's dreamscape. Utterly magical. One of the days produced the story *You, Me and the Stars* which you will find in Part IV. At the end of the story, we showered the story experiencers with hundreds of golden stars. At the end of the day, I swept up a handful from the floor. I keep them in places about my house – there is one in my handbag, one in a pot of pens and one in a box I use to carry sensory resources around. When I come across them I am transported back to the magic of that day. As I left I noticed other people doing the same, squirrelling stars away into pockets and handbags. I hope the magic carries to you through these pages.

PART II

SHARING SENSORY STORIES

Chapter 3

HOW TO SHARE A SENSORY STORY

Telling a sensory story is very simple; first you need to gather all the sensory stimuli you need for the story. Having a box designated to the story to keep your stimuli in is a great idea. To share the story, simply read each line and facilitate the accompanying experience. It may be that the experience is delivered at the end of the sentence or it might be delivered during the sentence, for example, on the particular word that relates to that stimuli. That is all there is to it!

This chapter provides detailed guidance about sharing sensory stories, but if you wish to download summary guidance for this, a free booklet is available from the sensory story page of: www.thesensoryprojects.co.uk.

MAINTAINING CONSISTENCY WHEN SHARING SENSORY STORIES

How you go about sharing a sensory story will depend very much on whom you are sharing it with. For some people, having a sensory story shared with them in a consistent manner can help them to develop their understanding, communication and expression of preferences. Repetition of a sensory story can relieve anxieties people may feel around sharing the story and so enable them to relax and interact with the stimuli more.

Sharing a sensory story in a consistent manner is still simply a case of reading the words and facilitating the stimuli; it is just that with consistent telling you will be aiming to read the words and facilitate the stimuli in the same way each time you deliver the story.[1]

---

[1] A short film (four minutes) on maintaining consistency is available to watch here: www. youtube. com/watch?v=reBMHoODr2s.

Here are a few of examples of why you might want to consider consistent sensory storytelling.

Example 1: Expressing preferences

I am telling a sensory story that involves two different smells. I make sure I deliver the smells in the same way each time I tell the story. The person I am sharing the story with always seems more interested in the floral scent than the citrus scent.

Their response communicates to me a preference for the floral scent. My close observation of their reaction to this stimulus allows me to hear them expressing that preference. I can use that information in the future on their behalf, for example if I were to go shopping to buy them shower gel, I would look for one with a floral scent.

If each time I tell the story I deliver the scents in different ways – perhaps making a big fuss out of one and holding it close to the person while just offering the other for a moment, or on some tellings, presenting the citrus scent in a prolonged and steady way but waving the floral scent back and forth beneath the person's nose – I won't know if their preference is for the scent or for the way I have delivered it.

Of course, this depends hugely on who is experiencing the story with you. You may be telling the story to someone who could tell you each time, 'I like this smell best.' For that person, if you vary how you deliver the experience this might be a way to keep the story interesting. The correct way to tell the story always depends on you and the person with whom you are sharing the story.

Example 2: Demonstrating learning

I am telling a sensory story that involves a loud noise. The sentence that precedes this noise is, 'She heard a bang.' I plan to tell this story every day for a week.

On Monday, I say, 'She heard a bang.' I make the sound. The story experiencer flinches at the sound and seems to smile. I observe their flinch and consider that it could count as a reaction.

On Tuesday, I say, 'She heard a bang.' I make the sound. The story experiencer flinches at the sound and smiles. I observe that their reaction is consistent with Monday's reaction. This is significant because it indicates to me that both the flinch and the smile are to do with the experience I am offering them. On Monday, the flinch might have been to the bang and the smile a reaction to a subsequent easing of some small pain caused by the movement of the flinch. I cannot know from one experience alone that the communication of that flinch is necessarily what I first presume it to be.

On Wednesday, I say, 'She heard a bang.' I make the sound. The story experiencer flinches at the sound and beams with enjoyment.

On Thursday, things happen just as they did on Monday, Tuesday and Wednesday, but on Friday something really interesting happens.

On Friday, I say, 'She heard a bang' and the story experiencer begins to smile before I have made the sound and their body tenses ready to flinch. I make the sound. They flinch and laugh. This pre-emptive response communicates to me that they knew what was going to happen next. That was their way of saying, 'I know what happens next in this story and I like it; this bit is my favourite part of this story.' They have demonstrated anticipation, which is a very exciting skill to witness in people who have often been written off as unable to learn.

Now consider a different version of events...

On Monday, I say, 'She heard a bang.' I make the sound. The story experiencer flinches and appears to smile. I think, 'Oh they like this bit!'

On Tuesday, I say, 'She heard a bang.' I make the sound several times. The story experiencer flinches smiles. I am thrilled with how much they are enjoying it.

On Wednesday, I am looking forward to this part of the story, I say, 'Ready? Here comes the good bit. She...heard...a...BANG!' I make the sound several times. The story experiencer flinches and laughs.

On Thursday, I am not able to tell the story so I ask someone else to tell it on my behalf. They say, 'She heard a bang', but they are worried about the noise that the stimulus might make so instead they pass it to the story experiencer to hold. The story experiencer does not react.

On Friday, I am able to tell the story and am looking forward to it. I say, 'She heard a bang', and go to make the sound but cannot find the stimulus as the person from the day before has put it away in a different place. Eventually I find it and make the noise. The story experiencer flinches and laughs.

In this second version of events the story experiencer has had a stimulating time. Chapter 1 on the importance of sensory stimulation showed that these experiences are valuable in and of themselves, but in this version of events the story experiencer has not been enabled to communicate their understanding of the story.

Consistency can be a very useful tool in sensory storytelling. If you are aiming for a high level of consistency, think about how you will achieve this. If it is likely that someone else will be telling the story as well, can you develop a system whereby you share in detail what you do and what responses you have observed? I am not recommending that *all* sensory experiences should be this consistently conducted – that would make for a very rigid and dull life. This is one way of sharing a sensory story and there are many others.

A researcher exploring the guidance given below for sharing sensory stories with adults with profound and multiple learning disabilities found that a consistent approach to sensory storytelling enhanced social interactions. There were examples such as that of a participant who after three repetitions of the story took the storyteller's hand and used it to interact with the stimuli. Another participant took the storyteller's hand on the fourth repetition of the story, and made eye contact with the storyteller on the fifth repetition. The frequency and duration of eye contact increased over subsequent tellings of the sensory story. Sharing in the story enhanced social interactions and strengthened bonds between the story experiencer and the storyteller (Grace and Silva 2017).

TIPS FOR CONSISTENT SHARING OF SENSORY STORIES

- Be prepared: prepare your resources and prepare your words.

- Take your time.

- Stick to the text.

- Know the person with whom you are sharing the story.

(The effectiveness of these tips was supported by research from Grace and Silva 2017.)

Be prepared
Telling a sensory story involves reading set sentences and facilitating sensory stimuli. In some situations, you will be taking it in turns between the reading and the facilitating; in others, you will be facilitating as you read. To be able to do this smoothly you need to have all your sensory stimuli laid out somewhere easy to reach. Stopping to find a particular stimulus, or to work out how to switch it on, will interrupt the flow of the story.

It is also a good idea to prepare yourself for reading a sensory story by reading it through out loud on your own first. This will give you a feel for how the words sound when you say them. We are all different and have different turns of phrase; if you feel a particular sentence does not work for you, or you will struggle to pronounce a particular word, change it beforehand rather than adapting as you go along. If someone else is going to be sharing the same sensory story with the same person then it can be a good idea to do this preparation together to ensure you will both be saying the same thing.

Once you have your wording and your stimuli organized think about how you will deliver them. Will a particular word be spoken loudly? Will you be facilitating a touch experience to someone's left or right side? Will a sight experience be presented up close or far away? There are lots of things to think about. It helps to know the person you plan to share the story with well so that you can facilitate the stimuli, and speak, in a way that best suits them.

Take your time

You may be able to rattle through the sentences and deliver the stimuli in just a few minutes, but this will not give the person you are sharing the story with a chance to absorb and respond to what is going on. I can best illustrate this point by drawing on an example from another communication strategy that is often used with people with profound and multiple learning disabilities: communication switches.

A communication switch is a large, easy-to-press button that can record a short message. People with profound and multiple learning disabilities can learn to press these switches; the hope is that the recorded voice can speak words that person would say if their physicality allowed them to. It is a great idea, but its success depends very much on how it is carried out. Here is an example from a classroom:

> *The teacher is delivering the register, calling each child's name in turn. Each child replies, 'Good morning'. When the teacher gets to the child with profound and multiple learning disabilities, the teaching assistant places a switch, on which is recorded 'Good morning' on their lap tray. The child does not respond, so the teaching assistant lifts the child's arm and places their hand on the switch, whereupon the switch says, 'Good morning,' and the teacher continues with the register.*

This physical assistance to operate the switch is not in itself bad practice. The child with profound and multiple learning disabilities will need to have the experience of pressing the switch a few times before they begin to understand what it does. Physical assistance teaches them that when they move their arm and place their hand on the switch, the switch says, 'Good morning.' However, if the physical assistance continues beyond the child learning this, communication is being squashed rather than facilitated.

Think about what is going on inside the child as they hear their name called in the register. At first, their brain must recognize that it is their name. They must then remember that they are expected to respond with, 'Good morning'. Once this is recalled, the brain must remember how to go about saying, 'Good morning'. Messages must be sent to the arm and to the hand to move. The arm and hand must act on these messages to move, and finally the switch will be pressed and will speak 'Good morning' on behalf of that child. All of this processing takes a long time and while it is going on the child seems to be doing nothing at all.

We are used to a flow of speech that is very brisk, and many people feel uncomfortable in long silences. If the child is given the time they need to respond then they are enabled to communicate. If someone lifts their hand and does it for them, they are prevented from communicating.

This example features a child, but the same would be true for an adult. Whatever age we are we need time to process information and respond, and for people with profound and multiple learning disabilities the time required to do this is likely to be different from the time you need to process and respond.

When we are facilitating sensory experiences within sensory stories we need to allow for this same processing time. A touch experience placed in the hand and then whisked away again might not be noticed. Someone who appears at first to not be responding may just be processing all the information they are receiving. Learn to feel comfortable in the pauses. Teach yourself to stay present with the person and the story (you may be in character) during these pauses. Watch the person with whom you are sharing the story closely for signs of response. For some people, these signs will be obvious: big body movements or loud vocalizations; for others, they may be far more subtle: a change in eye gaze or a relaxing of a small facial muscle. If you know the person well and watch them closely over time you will become accustomed to spotting their responses. Someone who is able to 'listen' to such subtle responses makes a great communication partner for a person with profound and multiple learning disabilities.

Stick to the text

Sticking to the text of the story means that your words become auditory cues for the sensory stimuli, enabling the person with whom you are sharing the story to know what is coming next. Consider again the example of a teacher calling the register that was mentioned earlier. The child in the example knew that when their name was called they were to say, 'Good morning'. Now suppose some days the teacher does not use names but simply says, 'Good morning' to each child in turn while looking at them, and on other days uses their surnames instead of their first names. In a situation where the auditory cue changes it is harder for the people to learn the expected response.

Keeping to the wording of the story sounds so easy to do, but it is easy to add in auditory padding or verbal prompting, for example when offering a smell experience: 'Mmm, doesn't that smell nice, can you smell that? Mmm, isn't it lovely?' or when offering a touch experience: 'Here, it is here, touch it with your hand, that's right, like this, can you feel it?' These verbal extras are often produced without thinking. They come naturally to us as people used to the speedy to and fro of conversation and aware of the awkwardness most people feel in silence. For people who struggle with verbal communication, a flurry of words can be confusing, can make it hard to pick out the important keyword and can overwhelm. This is not just a point to consider when sharing stories with someone who may need longer than average to process information; it is also one to bear in mind when sharing stories with someone who may find language difficult. Neurodivergent people, for example autistic people, often struggle to process language, so providing less language may make an experience more enjoyable for them. Once again, the right choice is all about understanding the person you are sharing the story with.

Choose what you will be saying ahead of sharing the story with someone, and stick to the text you have decided on. Feel comfortable in the silences; share them happily with the story experiencer and remain in the story as you do so. Think of other ways to offer any prompting that might be needed, for example gently guiding a person's hands towards a touch experience on the first telling of a story. Overall, hold back from what radio DJs would refer to as 'filling'.

Know the person with whom you are sharing the story

When sharing sensory stimuli with someone it is important to have some background knowledge on their sensory abilities, preferences and allergies. Clearly it is important not to give people taste experiences to which they are allergic. It also makes sense to facilitate a sound experience to the left ear of a person who has no hearing in their right ear. Knowing about people's sensory preferences can support you in facilitating the story in a more sympathetic way; for example, if you know that someone jumps easily at loud noises, you need not make the loud noise in a story at full volume.

It is quite easy for us to think we know a person well, but we may not realize what knowledge we are missing: you do not know what you do not know! This truism is exemplified by Vlaskamp and Cuppen-Fonteine's study

(2007): staff who supported adults with profound and multiple learning disabilities in a care home were observed offering a person the choice of whether to listen to music. This choice was offered by placing a music tape in front of the person – if they picked it up this was taken to mean they wanted to listen to music. If they did not pick up the tape staff took it to mean that they did not want to listen to music. The researchers found that in some situations the tape was being placed in a location where it was difficult for the person to see it. There are many variations in people's sight: some people will find it easier to see close up, others far off; some will be able to see moving objects but not static ones; people can have tunnel vision or impaired tunnel vision, only seeing things that are straight ahead of them or on the periphery of their vision.

Chapter 4

SENSORY STORIES FOR ALL

Complex Brains, Sensory Impairment and Epilepsy: Using Sensory
Stories with People with Profound and Multiple Learning Disabilities

At the time of writing, in the UK the term 'profound and multiple learning disabilities' is used to describe people who have multiple physical and
intellectual disabilities, often experiencing life without full access to sensory
information. The information in their brains can also be confused by epilepsy
shooting its lightning bolts across their neurological landscape. Life lived
through such complicated brains can be a confusing and disorientating
experience. If you support someone with profound and multiple learning
disabilities look up the freely available Core and Essential Service Standards
for Supporting People with Profound and Multiple Learning Disabilities
for a practical overview of best practice (Doukas *et al.* 2017). Sensory stories
can hold particular benefits for people with profound and multiple learning
disabilities and for other people who face multiple barriers to connecting
and engaging with life.

USING SENSORY STORIES TO SUPPORT PEOPLE WHO
FACE MULTIPLE BARRIERS TO ENGAGEMENT

Telling sensory stories consistently, using the tips from Chapter 3, will provide
someone who has profound and multiple learning disabilities with not only a
fun and stimulating range of sensory experiences, but also the opportunity to
communicate and demonstrate their learning and the chance to express their
opinions and preferences. The tips are all simple to implement, but, ironically,
they are as easy to get wrong as they are to get right. Research by ten Brug *et al.*
(2012) found that after a day's training, 84 per cent of those trained were able to
create sensory stories according to guidelines given by PAMIS, but only 1.3 per

cent went on to tell those stories correctly. It is easy to make sure you have all your sensory stimuli within reach before you begin to tell a story (tip 1) but it is equally easy to forget to check the battery on your torch. It is easy to take your time over telling a story (tip 2) but just as easy to rush to get it told before a TV programme starts. It is easy to read the sentences as they are written in the story (tip 3) but just as easy to add in extra comments of your own. Chapter 3 gives you a good understanding of why these simple tips are worth following when sharing a story with someone with profound and multiple learning disabilities. Of course, the very idea of there being a right and a wrong way to share a story between two people is a funny one; I hope that having read this book you will be able to find a way to share sensory stories that is right for you and right for the person with whom you are sharing them.

Chapter 3 described many of the benefits offered by sensory stories to people living lives through complex brains:

- Providing opportunities to express opinions.

- Enabling the sharer of the sensory story to listen to the preferences of the story experiencer.

- Providing a framework in which a person experiencing life through a complex brain can demonstrate their learning. This in turn can impact the understanding of those around them and so can be considered self-advocacy.

In this chapter, we are going to consider three more.

ORIENTATION

A person living through a complex brain, with limited access to sensory information, compromised by the presence of epilepsy or other illnesses, can find life a confusing experience. It is difficult to orientate oneself in the environment when faced with so many barriers to access.

Imagine what you would understand if you had limited access to sensory information, to memory, to understanding of the world and the processes within it. It is likely that much of life would swirl about you in a confusing soup of experience, but from time to time moments would make sense. The sound of a particular person's voice, the sensation of familiar fastenings around your body as you are hoisted from one location to another.

Having access to a set of clearly presented sensory experiences that repeat in a consistent manner can create a landscape in which someone living through a complex brain might be able to begin to orientate themselves within experience and be able to predict what will happen next. This in turn leads to the next benefit.

SENSE OF SELF AND TIME

When a person connects with a sensory experience it is not the experience alone that they experience, they also experience themselves. In that moment of feeling the roughness of bark on a tree there is both the knowing that the material beneath my hand is rough and the knowing of self as a person who feels roughness. Without this point of contact, both the self and the world are confusing and amorphous.

Within a sensory story, people are offered multiple points of contact with sensation. As their awareness of what comes next grows across multiple tellings of a sensory story and they begin to anticipate sensations, they are sensing time, and themselves within time. In the expectation of the next sentence of the story is the knowledge of the world and their continued presence in it.

CONFIDENCE

Moving on from these perhaps more philosophical supposed benefits of sensory stories in this segment we approach a very practical application. If I stripped you of your ability to understand the world and limited your access to sensory information about it and then confused matters further by having epilepsy attack your thoughts as you tried to make sense of them, it is likely that you would feel considerably more vulnerable in the world than you do right now. People living through complex brains often, rightly, feel this vulnerability, and unfamiliar circumstances or experiences can be distressing for them.

We can use sensory stories to target key experiences and so increase their access to the world and decrease their distress within it. This example illustrates what I am talking about:

I am walking along the seafront with a friend who has profound and multiple learning disabilities. My friend is enjoying the smell of the sea and feeling the warmth of the sun on their face as I wheel them along.

Suddenly a dog barks. My friend is frightened – this is a very natural, sensible response to a loud animal sound. The set of experiences my friend is going through have become alarming and our walk is no longer a pleasant experience.

If my friend had encountered the sounds of a dogs barking within the context of a sensory story, in an environment where they felt safe and secure, then they would recognize the sound and perhaps it would not be so alarming. Our walk could continue to be an enjoyable experience.

Experiencing a range of sensory stimuli within the security of a sensory story can support people to build their confidence at encountering new stimuli and open up the world to them.

Chapter 5

SENSORY PROCESSING DIFFERENCES

All of the information we receive comes to us through our senses, and to receive it we need two things: 1) working sense organs, 2) for the information that our sense organs deliver us to reach the brain at a level at which it can be taken in. An easy analogy for this is listening to music. When you listen to music you do so at a volume that is appropriate to you. If the sound is too quiet the strain of trying to hear it detracts from your ability to enjoy it. Likewise, if the sound is too loud the pain of it will overwhelm any enjoyment. And you probably remember a time in your teenage years when the 'right' volume of music was disputed in your household.

It is as if each of our senses has a volume control in our brain. For some people with sensory processing differences, or sensory processing disorder (I draw this distinction to acknowledge both those for whom a physiological difference in their brains causes this perceived difference and those for whom developmental experiences mean that their sensory processing is not where it is expected to be and is also perceived as being different), the volume controls on their senses are set in such a way as to not line up with the day-to-day experiences of life.

A person's sensory volume controls can be set too high, making the sensory world too much for them, or set too low, making it seem as though the world lacks stimulation, or they can be difficult to operate, so that the world lurches at first too loud, too bright, too rough, and then all of a sudden, not loud enough, not bright enough, not tactile enough.

Many people who have neurodivergent brains, for example autistic people, experience sensory processing differences. However, it is not necessary to have a neurodivergent condition in order to be deemed as having sensory processing differences (Owen *et al.* 2013). Dunn (1997, 2007) considered how a person's reaction to their sensory experience affects our ability to spot their difference and support their needs. People can react actively or passively. Someone who reacts actively will seek to do something about the imbalance they feel – either by blocking out stimuli they find too much or seeking to create stimulation where they do not feel they are getting enough. Someone who reacts passively will seek to endure the difference they experience. It is important to note that an active response from one person and a passive response from another does not mean that the active response person is suffering more. It is simply a different response to suffering.

This combination of, in Dunn's terminology, high/low neurological thresholds (in my analogy above these would be different settings on the volume controls) and active/passive responses produces four different manifestations of sensory processing differences.

High neurological threshold – passive response
Someone with a high neurological threshold who responds in a passive way will appear bored, aloof and disengaged with the world around them.

Low neurological threshold – passive response
Someone with a low neurological threshold who responds in a passive way will seem uncomfortable, distracted and slightly distressed.

High neurological threshold – active response
Someone with a high neurological threshold and an active response will seek to find sensory stimulation in their environment; people can be very creative in how they go about doing this. I have known people to empty bathroom products completely and smear them around (lots of smell and touch experiences). Responses like this, although catastrophic to a tidy home, can be quite funny; however, people may also self-harm or harm others to gain stimulation, which can cause a great deal of distress and is in turn indicative of how distressing sensory differences can be for those who experience them.

Low neurological threshold – active response
Someone with a low neurological threshold and an active response will seek to block out the stimulation they find overwhelming. Strategies such as closing eyes, turning away and blocking ears can all be utilized to block out stimulation. Some people find they cannot tolerate the feel of clothing against their skin and so remove it or select particular clothing, for example items without seams. In extreme cases, people may turn to self-harm, for example

hitting their ears or their heads, in an attempt to shut everything out. It is important to recognize that this is not a disproportionate response to a sound, or sensation, or whatever the sensory experience happens to be, but it is an accurate reporting of how upsetting that experience is for that person.

People with an active response to their sensory processing difficulties tend to be easier to spot than people with passive responses. It is good to be mindful when supporting people that sensory processing differences may play a role in behaviour. Although it is not easy to spot the passive responders, if you have an awareness of sensory processing differences you may be able to spot changes in a person's responses based on location. For example, I once met a person who only talked when it was dark. Those closest to that person thought that while it was light they felt too overwhelmed to speak, but in darkness, with the associated lack of visual stimulation, they were able to relax and communicate.

USING SENSORY STORIES TO SUPPORT PEOPLE WHO EXPERIENCE SENSORY PROCESSING DIFFERENCES

People with sensory processing differences benefit from sharing sensory stories in two ways that are specific to them, as well as in the other ways discussed in this book:

1. Sensory stories can give them the opportunity to encounter and get used to stimuli.

2. Sensory stories can present them with the opportunity to practise their responses to stimuli.

People with sensory processing differences can struggle with eating, and sensory stories have a role to play in supporting them to meet the challenge food can pose.

The following three sections discuss these benefits in more detail. If you are sharing sensory stories with people with sensory processing differences, you may also find that many of the tips for consistent storytelling in Chapter 3 will be useful.

Sensory stories as a way of introducing, and becoming accustomed to, stimuli

It is natural for us to be wary of new experiences. We do not know whether they are safe and our instinctual caution protects us from spontaneously tasting that funny coloured mushroom or reaching into the brightly flickering flame. We are all a little bit anxious of encountering new sensory experiences: how do you feel about touching that slug or holding that spider? What about tasting an oyster for the first time or sniffing stinky tofu? It is also natural for us to find some sensory experiences overwhelming: music that is just too loud, the sound of fingers down a chalkboard, and so on.

Nature has ways of letting us know that new experiences are safe. If we see someone else have an experience and nothing bad happens, we begin to think we might be okay to have the same experience. We know we should try a little bit of something first and wait to see if anything bad happens before trying more. We are able to educate our palates to like tastes we initially disliked; this is a process of learning that the taste is safe. Many coffee drinkers will know that when they first tasted coffee they found it bitter and unpleasant, but once they had learned to like the flavour they never looked back. We can create a similar progression of experiences for someone encountering sensory stimuli in the context of a sensory story.

For people with sensory processing differences, the opportunity to regularly encounter new sensory stimuli through repeated telling of a sensory story can allow them to grow accustomed to those stimuli and not feel overwhelmed by them. Some stimuli may even come to be enjoyed.

Using a sensory story to facilitate these encounters is beneficial, as the story element wraps the process up in fun while also providing reassurance about what is going to happen next. Once the story is familiar it will feel safe, and the lack of surprises will be relaxing and enjoyable.

Regular exposure to a range of sensory stimulation can help people with high neurological thresholds to modulate their sensory systems so that they are more receptive to the stimulation found in daily life.

Your approach when sharing a sensory story with a person with sensory processing difference who has a low neurological threshold will very much depend on that person and what they are willing to experience and can tolerate. You will need to decide how many new experiences to allow in a story and how best to facilitate those experiences.

You can present a chosen new sensory experience in the same way on each retelling of the story. The benefit of this is that it becomes very predictable and the person experiencing the story knows exactly what is going to happen. You would, in this instance, be looking for more interaction with the stimuli from the story experiencer on each subsequent telling of the story. For the story to be successful, the person with sensory processing differences needs to find it a safe and enjoyable place, so avoid putting pressure on them to interact with stimuli. A little prompting or encouragement may be supportive; perhaps you can share the story with two people at once and have the second person really enjoy the interactions with the stimuli as a way of tempting the person with sensory processing differences to have a go. We are bolder and braver within the storytelling context, so a timid story experiencer might surprise you.

A second option is to grade the stimuli that you are expecting the story experiencer to interact with; this could also be done in reverse for people with high neurological thresholds. In the case of a person with a low neurological threshold, you might begin by not expecting them to interact with the stimuli at all but merely watch someone else's interaction. In subsequent tellings of the story, you would be looking for them to interact with a weakened version of the stimuli. Over future tellings, you would gradually increase the stimuli until the final telling has the person experiencing the stimuli at full strength. For a story experiencer with a high neurological threshold, you could begin with an exaggerated version of the stimuli and over retellings dilute it down to a subtler stimulus.

Sensory stories as a way to rehearse responses to stimuli

We should not expect everyone to be able to cope with every sensory experience – no one has this expected of them in life. Personally, I find music in nightclubs too loud, mushrooms too slippery and dog poo too smelly; I do not expect these sensory preferences to change. It is unrealistic to think that through practice a person with sensory processing differences will be able to master every sensory experience they encounter.

If you believe that the story experiencer is not going to be able to learn to tolerate an experience then you have a decision to make: is it an experience they must have? Ask yourself: is it an experience that they will come across in life? Would avoiding that experience impact negatively on their life? If it is an experience that is a necessary part of a balanced life then your aim is to teach them how to deal with and respond to the experience when it happens. If it is an experience that can be avoided without damaging their life then your aim is to teach them appropriate ways of avoiding it.

We all have sensory experiences we dislike; knowing how to avoid them or how to respond appropriately are important skills to learn. Here are a couple of examples.

Fingers down a chalkboard

Imagine that the first time I hear this sound I am a baby – the noise upsets me and so I scream and cry. The next time I encounter this sound I have reached my terrible twos – this time I shout and hit the person making the noise. I get a little older and a little wiser and when I next hear the sound I am able to put my fingers in my ears and block it out. A little older and a little wiser still with a few extra social skills and next time I encounter the sound I am able to ask the person making it whether they could please stop as I find the noise unpleasant.

You can see in this example that there is a progression to my responses. I have not made progress in terms of how difficult I find the sensation, I have made progress in my understanding of what I can do about the difficult sensation. The opportunity for me to encounter a stimulus within the context of a sensory story on repeated occasions gives me the chance to practise more sophisticated reactions to that stimulus.

Mushrooms

I dislike the taste of mushrooms and I can avoid them. I make choices in restaurants that do not involve mushrooms; I pick them out of my food (when no one is looking); I choose not to buy them in the shops. These things might limit my life experiences a little and they might be a little impolite, but they are not going to significantly impact my life. I have learned to cope with my dislike of mushrooms.

If I hadn't managed to acquire these coping strategies, the opportunity to encounter mushrooms within the safety of a story and not be required to eat them, but instead be given strategies to inform my reactions, would be very valuable to me.

In some cases, we may be able to teach people with sensory processing differences strategies for avoiding stimuli they cannot tolerate (like showing me how to pick mushrooms out of my food). In other cases, we may be looking to teach them ways of coping with the unpleasantness of having those experiences (like showing me how to put my fingers in my ears in response to an unpleasant sound).

Sensory stories can be a first step in identifying experiences that people find hard to cope with. They can also provide a place to practise reactions to stimuli where getting it wrong will not be as catastrophic as in real life. It can help to make story experiencers aware of their reactions. Talking about a reaction can help the story experiencer become self-aware and manage their responses. Recording reactions on each telling of a story can help story experiencers feel a sense of progress. Even if progress is made in very small steps, having a record can help – you can point to small changes and express your expectation that more changes will occur, as well as your confidence in them to be able to make those changes (a recording method like those illustrated in Chapter 9 would suit this process). Together you can pick a goal to work towards, for example, 'I will see a mushroom and be able to feel calm, I will not need to scream.' Setting such a goal and recording the steps taken to reach it will help the story experiencer to feel that it is going to happen.

Some sensory experiences are necessary for life – necessary for our survival (such as eating). When a person with sensory processing difficulties struggles with a necessary life experience it can be very distressing for them and their loved ones. Sensory stories provide a simple way of helping people with sensory processing differences to encounter and cope with a wide range of sensory experiences.

The role of sensory stories in addressing eating difficulties

Eating is a very sensory-rich experience. If you find eating overwhelming and distressing, this is going to impact your life in a negative way. Learning to avoid eating is not an option; the only option is a gradual process of learning to process all the sensations involved.[1] The most important thing when supporting a person with a difficulty like this is to maintain a low-pressure environment. Addressing the difficulty at a time that is not a mealtime, in a context different to mealtimes, is a good first step. Try to identify which aspect of eating the person is struggling with. Is it the smell of the food? Is it the consistency or texture? You may be able to answer these questions by observing their reactions to other sensory stimuli they encounter during sensory storytelling sessions. They might be happy touching sticky substances but resistant to smelling strong smells.

Building up a picture of a person's sensory preferences is instrumental in helping them to progress and develop.

Once you have identified the specifics of the problem, you can begin to address it. If you cannot identify a specific problem and believe all aspects of eating to be challenging then you can address them one by one. Take eating as a touch experience as an example: young infants often lift objects to their mouths to touch them; this is because the lips and tongue are very sensitive to touch and so they are able to get detailed information about an object by touching it with their mouths. If you are someone who struggles with touch then touching with your mouth is going to be very difficult. You can start by getting used to touching things with your hands or even feet. Being offered

---

[1]   It is important to recognize that eating difficulties can be caused by many different things. If someone you love is struggling to eat, ensure they get the right medical attention to find out the cause of the difficulty.

food substances to be touched and explored without the pressure of having to eat them gives a person the chance to build up familiarity with what they are feeling. Once they are able to touch something with their hands, they can begin to try touching it with their mouths. You may have to begin with non-food substances – do not worry; just gradually increase the diversity of textures encountered and work towards touching food. Make these explorations playful and fun, introduce silliness and humour to signal that there is no pressure, just a sensation to experience if and when they are ready to.

There is no one solution; progression will be specific to each person and their particular abilities and struggles. Think about building up the component parts of eating: can they touch food substances? Can they smell food smells? Can they hear eating sounds? Some people find it easier to cope with the sensations of eating when some aspects are removed, for example they may find it easier to eat if they hold their nose to eliminate smell from the equation, or if they listen to music at the same time to mask the sounds of eating.

The most important thing, and equally the hardest thing to do, is to allow the sensory journey to be one without pressure. Just share the story and enjoy it. Allow progress to happen naturally, however slow that might be. Once you feel progress has been made, you can begin to make the transition between story and real-life application – a starting step could be to tell the story at the dinner table (not at dinner time); another step could be to start telling stories about food, for example the *Seasoned with Spice* story in this book.

Often the conversation around eating becomes very binary, 'Did they eat it or didn't they?' and the apparent failure in the 'no' response is very damaging to a person and to those who love them. By considering the sensory aspects of eating we can shift this from a yes/no situation to a pathway. Instead of 'No they did not eat' we can say, 'They smelt three different food smells today, and touched two food substances.' We can celebrate successes!

Chapter 6

USING SENSORY STORIES...

Sensory stories are great for sharing with people regardless of disability, ability or neurodivergence, as the added sensory stimulus supports engagement and memory and just makes the story-sharing experience more fun. When I deliver training days on sensory stories I always tell a sensory story and a non-sensory story to the delegates. People find it easier to remember the sensory story; they find it more interesting. I could present an endless list of different conditions for which sensory stories have relevance, but that would make for rather a dull read and there would always be groups I had missed from the list. Instead, I have opted to highlight the specific benefits sensory stories hold for people with different challenges. It is by no means an exhaustive list; I hope that reading this book will provide you with the knowledge and insight you need to discern whether the stories hold any specific benefits for the people you know.

...TO SUPPORT PEOPLE WHO EXPERIENCE INFORMATION OVERLOAD, SUCH AS LANGUAGE PROCESSING, SENSORY PROCESSING

The sparseness of the language within a sensory story can make the information conveyed by that story easier for people who find verbal communication difficult to take on-board. When someone does not understand an idea or a concept our tendency is to explain more – to add language until we have explained the concept in as many ways as possible. This verbal approach to understanding can be difficult for people struggling with verbal communication to contend with. In a sensory story the stimuli act as an explanation and can help a person understand what is being conveyed by the story.

Autistic people often experience sensory processing differences. Coping with these differences can use up cognitive capacity that, were their sensory environment less challenging, could be used for other endeavours.

Imagine that a person's total cognitive capacity – that is, all the space they have in their brain for thinking – is represented by the large square in Figure 6.1. The small square inside the left-hand large square represents how much space is taken up in the average mind by processing sensory information. You can see there is a lot of space left over for other activities. The large square in Figure 6.1 represents what the mind of someone with sensory processing difficulties might be like. If more space is taken up by processing sensory information then there is less space left over for other tasks. This visual representation is good for conceiving information overload of various kinds. You could also think of the smaller squares as the space taken up in the mind by processing language or coping with anxiety. Both squares represent people who are coping with their experience; if the inner squares were to eclipse the outer squares, that would represent someone who was not coping, such a person might express their overwhelm by going into meltdown or shutdown.

Figure 6.1 A representation of cognitive capacity

People may benefit from the opportunity to encounter and become accustomed to sensory stimuli presented by sensory stories in the same way as people with sensory processing differences. Information conveyed in a concise way, as happens within sensory stories, is easier to take in than language-rich information. Most people find concepts explained through sensory media easier to understand than those explained with language alone, for example, in my sensory story *The Birth of a Star*, gas is described as spinning. The word spinning is accompanied by a visual experience of something spinning. It is much easier to understand what the word spinning means when you are watching something spin. For people who struggle with processing language, as can happen for autistic people, the non-verbal explanation provided by sensory stimuli can support understanding.

The section on inspiring interaction in Chapter 7 may hold particular relevance for those wishing to share sensory stories with autistic people.

...TO SUPPORT CONCENTRATION

For those of us who find concentrating relatively straightforward, it can be easy to view concentration as having just a few components; for example, as you read this book you are concentrating because you are looking at the page and reading the words.

In a classroom, a child might be considered to be concentrating because they are looking at the teacher and not talking. In fact, these identifying characteristics of a concentrating person are only the last few steps of a series of skills that have to be mastered along the road to concentration.

I expect as you read this book you are sitting on a chair; perhaps you've been sitting for quite some time. One of the skills you have is the ability to sit still in one place – to tolerate how it feels as the circulation in your body adjusts to that sitting – perhaps your bum has gone numb. You can imagine that a child sitting cross-legged on a classroom carpet has to contend with the feeling of their ankle bones pressing into the floor; they also have to ward off other sensory distractions, for example noises outside the classroom, pictures on the wall and the fidgeting of other children. If you are not initially able to concentrate then you move, and you do not get the chance to develop those underlying skills, such as the ability to sit still.

We know that some things are easier to concentrate on than others. If I were to stand before you and lecture at you for two hours in a monotone, you would find it hard to concentrate, whether or not the content of what I was saying was interesting. However, if I sit you in a cinema and ask you to concentrate for two hours, you would likely find it easy.

Sensory stories offer people something to hang their concentration on – they have something to listen to, touch, smell, and so on. It is easier for them to sit and listen to a sensory story than it is for them to listen to a typical story. That experience of concentrating gives people the opportunity to practise all the skills involved in concentration. It is not that they must always have information presented in such a stimulating way, but that by presenting information in a way that makes it easy for them to concentrate you are giving them the opportunity to develop the underlying skills of concentration that they can draw on later in less stimulating situations.

...TO ENGAGE PEOPLE WITH REDUCED SENSORY CAPACITY

If one or more of your senses does not function fully then having access to information via your other senses is very important. It is a mistake to think that sensory stories will not be suitable for someone who is, for example, blind or deaf because they involve sight experiences or sound experiences. If someone is completely blind then sight experiences will need to be substituted with an alternative experience – a story such as *Seasoned with Spice* would be ideal for sharing with a blind person. There is always scope for swapping experiences to make a story more relevant to a particular experiencer. Total sensory loss is relatively rare – many people will experience a reduction in capacity – so related sensory experience may still be appropriate. A strong sight experience may suit someone with partial sight loss, as it will be a visual experience they can access.

The broad range of sensory stories means that there is a wide palette of experiences for people with reduced sensory capacity to access. When I am asked about the possibility of using sensory stories with people with reduced sensory capacity I often think about an experience I had early on in my teaching career.

My school allowed me to observe various outside practitioners who came into the school to work with our people so that I could learn from what they did. I remember watching a young man who was totally blind reading to a specialist Braille practitioner in a one-to-one session. His task was to read the Braille on the page and also to extract information from the accompanying tactile picture. This picture was an exact replica of the picture in the book, but made out of vacuum-formed plastic so that what were lines in the book were ridges in the plastic and colours in the book were textures in the plastic. The picture was of a child playing on a swing. The young man read the Braille text successfully and answered questions on it with enthusiasm. He was then asked to identify which piece of playground equipment the child in the story was playing on. This information was only available in the picture. He half-heartedly put his hand on the plastic and then shrugged and said, 'I dunno.'

The touch experience of a piece of bumpy plastic is not a great one; it feels much the same as the plastic wrapping on toys or the lid of one's packed lunchbox – it was not an interesting touch for him. This particular young man had been blind from birth; the lines representing the swing meant nothing to him as they represented a visual world. Had he lost his sight then the lines might have meant something to him. In his world, a swing was the feel of the rope or chain that held it up, the movement of the seat and the feel of the wind on his face. I hope that if he had been reading a sensory story on the same topic, the accompanying touch experience would have been an engaging one for him.

…TO SUPPORT SPEECH

People who find verbal communication difficult for whatever reason – a stutter, nerves, an enlarged tongue or other physical difference – benefit from lots of practice at verbalizing. However, many people who experience difficulties in enunciating words become self-conscious about trying to speak and end up speaking less, not more, than normal. Extra support to be understood can give a person with speech difficulties the boost of confidence they need in order to have a go at verbalising. As with the above example, signs and symbols can help, as can sensory stimuli. Consider a story with the words 'bright blue light' within it. A person who finds sounds difficult to articulate may pronounce this as 'ight ooo ight'. If they are asked simply to speak the words they may be hesitant to do so, knowing that 'ight ooo ight' will be hard for others to understand. However, if they are to facilitate the stimulus of a bright blue light as they say 'ight ooo ight' they will have added confidence in their being understood. Using the stimulus to support their communication means that the person is more likely to be understood when they speak and so get the encouraging feedback of being understood, which will give them more confidence to try verbalizing again in the future.

Sensory stimuli can also be used by people with communication difficulties to answer questions about stories without having to verbalize at all. Access to narrative should not be contingent on a person's particular disability. Language users tend to hope that everyone will be able people who speak confidently and clearly. We would never make access to narrative contingent on one's ability to walk, and we should not make it contingent on people being able to speak. Taking part in sensory stories allows people to build an understanding of the turn-taking nature of communication. Using sensory stimuli, people can answer questions about a story, such as, 'What comes next?' and 'Which was your favourite part?' They can demonstrate their recall of the story by facilitating the stimuli in the correct order. Having an alternative means to communicate means we do not impose barriers to communication and literacy skills based on mastering the skill of language.

...TO SUPPORT MEMORY

When we learn in a multi-sensory way, more of our brain is engaged in learning. For someone with memory difficulties, having more of the brain engaged in a task gives them more chance of being able to remember the task. It also gives them more avenues to their memory. For example, if I had read you a typical story called *Starshine* in which a boy goes on an adventure to the stars, I might ask you about it the following day. I might ask you if you remember the story by using its name, 'Do you remember *Starshine*?' I might try describing what happens, 'Do you remember the boy going on a journey?' and so on. Although I am approaching the memory in different ways, I am actually only giving you one sort of prompt: a verbal one. If I had read you *The Birth of a Star* I could ask if you remembered it by name, but I could also ask through repeating one of the stimuli to see if you appeared to recognize the experience.

Sensory stories provide information in a multi-sensory way; when repeated in a consistent way they can be easier for people with memory difficulties to remember than typical stories. The sensory stimulation within the stories supports the creation of memories.

People with learning disabilities may find laying down new memories difficult (Boucher and Bowler 2011; Jarrold *et al.* 2008; Lacey 2009; Swanson 1993). Someone with a learning disability may be able to fully engage in, and enjoy, new experiences, but that will not necessarily mean they can remember them later.

Creating a sensory story out of an event gives you a tool that you can use to reinforce memories of what happened. Imagine a trip to a swimming pool: during the trip, you will experience handing over money and being given a rubber wrist band, changing into your swimming costume while standing on ridged plastic mats, swimming – with the smell of chlorine and the sound of others splashing – having a hot shower and putting your wet swimming costume into a plastic bag. As each of these things occur you can take a moment to make everyone on the trip aware of them and make sure everyone has the experience; for example, by allowing each person to pay for their swim personally rather than paying for the group as a whole. You should clearly label each activity as it happens: 'We are paying for our swim and being given a wrist band.' You should collect resources that will allow you to facilitate the experiences again when back at your base, such as asking the swimming pool if you can keep a wrist band or taking a sample of pool water home with you. When you are back at your base you will be able to repeat the experiences and retell the event using the resources you collected. For example, 'We went to the swimming pool and paid to swim' – experiencing handing over money, 'We were given a wrist band' – experiencing putting on a wrist band, and so on. By repeating the account and the experiences you will help your experiencers to remember the activity.

Sharing the sensory experiences again after the experience can be a way for people to 'talk' about their experiences, something we all love to do, whether we are users of language or not – we all love to tell stories from our own lives.

Dr Nicola Grove's work at the OpenStoryTeller's Project and through the Surviving Through Story Project (2020) compellingly illustrates the power of being able to tell one's own stories for people with learning disabilities and neurodivergent conditions.

...TO SUPPORT PEOPLE EXPERIENCING MENTAL ILL-HEALTH

When we experience mental ill-health we can seek to withdraw from the world. Life can become overwhelming and human contact too much to cope with. In this respect, we can be very similar to someone with sensory processing differences who has a low neurological threshold. Gently exploring a sensory story with a person experiencing mental ill-health can encourage them to re-engage with life.

A connection with sensation can act like a little piece of mindfulness in motion, a connection to the present, to the security of the here and now.

Sensory stimuli can be very emotive; for example, particular smells may bring back strong memories, or particular touches may be comforting. When sharing a sensory story with someone experiencing mental ill-health, allow space for them to explore their emotional response to the stimuli.

Chapter 3 explains how to share a sensory story in a consistent manner. It may be that if a person experiencing mental ill-health is feeling particularly vulnerable, the familiarity and predictability brought about by consistent repetition of a story can be soothing.

PART III

USING SENSORY STORIES AS A BASIS FOR ENGAGING AND INTERACTIVE SESSIONS

Chapter 7

SUPPORTING LEARNING AND DEVELOPMENT

INSPIRING INTERACTION

Communication can be a very daunting experience for some people. The concentration of information and intensity of social contact that is involved in standard communication can be overwhelming. It is natural for people to avoid situations that feel overwhelming to them; being forced to take part only serves to exacerbate the anxiety they feel. Sensory stories can be used to encourage, even tempt, people into communicating. The use of sensory stimuli to convey meaning within a sensory story means that there is less pressure on the text to convey everything. The smaller word count of a sensory story when compared with a typical story may mean that people who find spoken communication difficult will find a sensory story easier to engage with.

A proactive way of using sensory stories to engage people in communication is to make them a desirable experience or the object of curiosity. Here is a technique you might like to try.

1. Store the sensory stimuli needed for your story in a fabulous-looking box; if you are creative, make one.

2. Arrange a situation whereby you, the box and the person you hope to engage in communication are all in the same place, ideally somewhere relatively bland so that the box is the most interesting thing.

3. Have in mind a particular set of conditions, relevant to the person with whom you will be sharing the story, that will form the basis of a communication contract between the two of you. It might be that they will sit down, or touch the box, or look towards you. The conditions you come up with agree between the two of you what is to be

involved in communication. If you are happy to share a sensory story with someone who is simultaneously watching TV or climbing on furniture then you are saying that to do these things while communicating with you is okay. You do not have to formulate conditions that represent standard communication, but you may build on your contract over time in a way that tends towards more standard expectations of communication. At first, you might look for them simply to look towards what is happening but not come near, or you may want them to stop vocalizing in order to let you speak but be happy for them to roam around while you speak. Later on, you might look to adjust your contract.

4. Sit in a relaxed fashion yourself and look interested in the box; you could even peek inside. You are aiming to excite their curiosity about what is in the box.

5. When the personalized conditions of your communication contract are met, open the box and begin sharing the story.

6. Stop sharing the story as soon as the conditions are no longer being met. Doing this allows the other person to give and retract consent with regards to taking part in communication.

7. Restart if the conditions are met. (Imagine you have a 'pause' button.)

This stopping and starting enables the person with whom you wish to communicate to control how much communication they experience. Having control over the situation will lessen their anxiety about taking part. Over time, you can build on your communication contract. In this way, you can both enjoy sharing the story together.

Chapter 8

STRUCTURING SESSIONS TO CHALLENGE AND INCLUDE A RANGE OF PEOPLE

In an ideal world, you will be able to share a sensory story on a one-to-one basis with the story experiencer. However, very few of us operate in an ideal world. Sensory stories can be used as a structure to build engaging experiences around; using the stories in this way can enable you to include a range of people in a shared experience.

CREATING SENSORY ACCESSIBILITY

For some people, new sensory experiences associated with new places or activities can be alarmingly unfamiliar. If you do not know where you are, if you do not know what is happening, then the associated anxiety can form a barrier to a potentially enjoyable experience. Sensory stories can be used or cue people into experiences they may have, taking the anxiety out of these experiences and creating sensory accessibility to them.

To view a short film about sensory accessibility visit: https://youtu.be/hN8zRsWvqZA.

To watch a short film featuring myself and my friend Rosa using a sensory accessibility story to support Rosa in accessing the circus visit: www.youtube.com/watch?v=HfFU9wVH8Hk&t=1s.

I have enjoyed creating sensory access stories for all sorts of places. The Palace tour of the King's State Apartments at Kensington Palace is a great example of a sensory story that can be used to prepare people for an experience. The experience of entering the Palace – the grandeur of the building, the richness of the colours of the walls and the paintings and the sound quality produced by the high ceilings and bare floors – is a very different experience from entering most rooms we frequent on a daily basis. Changes to what we are used to produce anxiety and this can be heightened for people who process sensory information differently.

The sensory tour of Kensington Palace has ten parts, each of which relates to a location within the King's State Apartments. Each location has a short sentence or phrase that explains an aspect of history and has an associated sensory experience.

The sensory tour leads people through the experiences they can expect when they reach the Palace. Sharing the tour before their visit gives people the opportunity to build up an understanding of what they will encounter, so when they arrive their anxiety about the unfamiliar place is reduced. The tour can then be used within the Palace and has the same phrases and experiences as the one they experienced in preparation. Delivered in situ, the experiences are bigger and richer, allowing people to experience awe in response to the remarkable rooms of the King's State Apartments.

INSPIRING CREATIVE WRITING
Creative writing challenges

You can use sensory stories as a stimulus for creative writing. Share a sensory story with your students so that they are familiar with what constitutes a sensory story.

Ask your students to make a sensory plan for their creative writing

Have your students think of a story they plan to write. This can be a story of their own creating or a story based on a familiar narrative. Ask them to write the title of the story in the centre of a page, and on radial lines around it write down each of the senses. They must then think of the sensory experiences that might be had within that story and write all their ideas down next to their associated sense. Once they have completed this plan they can write their story. This should lead to a beautiful piece of descriptive writing enriched with sensory detail.

Create a story based on a sensory sequence

Present your students with a sequence of sensory experiences. Before sharing the experiences, tell them that they are going to write a story based on what they experience. Students must take in each experience and use their imaginations to think of what could be happening in the story to create that experience. Leave the stimuli laid out in sequential order for your students to re-experience as needed during their writing. This should result in some extraordinary pieces of imaginative writing.

Create a story based on sensory prompts

Give people a selection of sensory stimuli and ask them to spend some time experiencing them and thinking about how they could be used within a story. They must then create a story based on the experiences – they can use the experiences in any order and do not have to make use of all those offered.

Distillation

Condensing a story down into ten sentences or fewer requires a high level of comprehension skills. To do this, a person must be able to identify: the key plot points in a story; the main characters; the central message or moral of the story; the genre of the story. People must make tough judgements about what is essential to the narrative and what is not. Deciding what to leave out of a story is a high-level comprehension skill.

When you tell people you want them to write a story in 'just' ten sentences they will think you are giving them an easy task and be happy to tackle it. Allow them plenty of time for the discussions they will need to have in order to decide what those ten sentences will be.

The ability to distil a large amount of information into a few phrases is a great revision skill. Once your students have their ten sentences you can ask them to think of sensory experiences for each sentence. Linking the sentences to sensory experiences will make them more memorable, so it is likely that people will be able to memorize their ten-sentence version of the story. If a lot of thought has gone into deciding what those ten sentences are, in remembering the ten sentences they will probably be able to expand them to cover the important parts of the original story.

This activity does not need to be restricted to English literature; you can ask your students to summarize the content of their latest science module in ten sentences or to distil a historical story into ten sentences.

BOOKENDING

Sensory stories have very few words but a lot of content. The content of sensory stories can be expanded on to engage a range of people. Take the story *Seasoned with Spice* as an example. This story is about cooking, and people could be expected to:

- experience cooking facilitated by someone else

- help out with cooking in small ways, for example by stirring a mixture

- follow a basic recipe themselves

- comment on an item as it is being cooked

- compare two recipes and pick the best

- design their own recipe

- create a recipe to serve a particular purpose, for example a healthy cake recipe.

These activities cover a wide range of abilities, but they are all about cooking and all directly relate to the story.

Bookending a session with a sensory story involves telling the story at the beginning and the end of the session and providing activities at a level appropriate to the people experiencing the story. It can also support the mind in organizing the information gained within those sessions. Knowing where information is stored in the mind helps us to retrieve that information in future; for example, if you ask me to multiply seven by nine, I know you are asking me a maths question and mentally I reach for the parts of my brain that deal with maths.

Language is the primary way information is organized within the mind. Our minds undergo structural changes when we acquire language, almost as if they are big filing cabinets, and language enables us to label the pockets within them. For people who do not have this filing system in place, providing structure through sequenced sensory experiences is a way of supporting their ability to retain and recall information.

Sharing a sensory story at the start of a session is a good way of introducing a topic and providing an overview of what that session is going to be about. Sharing the sensory story at the end of a session allows people time to reflect on their learning and fit it into the context of the bigger picture supplied by the sensory story.

Repeating the story over time is likely to result in people memorizing the story. The story can then be used as an aide-memoire for all the learning that took place within the sessions bookended by the story.

BUILDING

You can build up a sensory story over a series of sessions with people. In session one you might share only the first couple of sentences of the story, allowing the people experiencing the story to explore the associated sensory stimuli and then complete a learning task based on those sentences. At the end of the session you would revisit those sentences. You can choose between asking story experiencers to predict what might come next in the story or sharing the next few lines as a preview of the following session.

Building has many of the benefits of bookending; the main difference is that people do not hear the full story until the final sessions in the series, meaning that it can be slightly harder for them to memorize the whole story.

However, not telling the whole story all at once allows for people to predict, and to wonder about, what will come next and prevents them from getting bored with hearing the same story repeatedly. The choice between building or bookending with a sensory story will depend on the people you are sharing the story with: will they need the repetition that comes from hearing the whole story every session? Will they be drawn in by wondering what happens next in a story that builds over time?

Chapter 9

A NIFTY ASSESSMENT TOOL

You do not fatten a pig by weighing it: progress is made whether or not it is measured. However, doing a little assessment can help us to fine tune our sensory story sharing and it is especially useful for deciding when to start telling a new story.

Assessment can be a requirement of a particular job role; it can be useful in justifying the expenditure of time and money on sensory stories, and it can provide cause for the celebration of achievements. Keeping track of how a person is responding when you share a sensory story can help you to build up a picture of their sensory abilities and preferences, which can then be used as a tool for them to self-advocate.

The method I am going to share with you here is simple, quick and purposeful.

If you would like to watch me describe this method, rather than read it, you can view a short webinar at www.callscotland.org.uk/professional-learning/webinars/WEB191; if you want an easy way of sharing this method with others then the photo album at https://tinyurl.com/yzxw75jb can help.

ENGAGEMENT WITH SENSORY STORIES

Create a simple chart with an X and Y axis. The X axis is going to represent sections of the story so divide this by how many sections your story has, for example an eight-sentence story will have an X axis divided into eight sections. Your Y axis is for the person's responses to the stimulus and story.

Keep the chart alongside you as you tell the story. If the person you are sharing the story with appears to respond to a particular stimulus, make a mark on the chart that relates to that response. A mark positioned high against the Y axis indicates a big response, a mark positioned low indicates a mild response. (If you want, you can extend the Y axis below the X axis and use it to indicate positive and negative responses.)

When you first tell the story, you can expect to see just one or two marks on your chart. Make a chart for each time you tell the story. Over time you can hope to see the number of marks on your chart increasing, and creeping up the Y axis, building a picture of engagement.

When you begin to see the number of marks on the chart decreasing, it is time to start thinking about telling a new story.

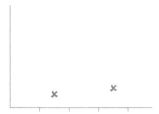

Figure 9.1: Reactions chart

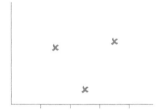

Figure 9.2: Completed reactions chart

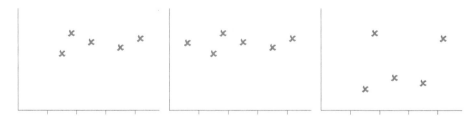

Figures 9.3, 4 and 5: Responses over time

This system of recording engagement with sensory stories is very efficient to both run and to read. You could, of course, write short descriptive sentences at the end of each session describing the responses you saw (you can always add notes to charts if you want this detail), but to get the information from them they would have to be read through. However, to get the information from the chart, all you have to do is glance at it.

Picture a number of these charts laid out on a page or on the floor, with the chart relating to the first time someone experienced the story at the top, and the chart relating to the most recent time someone experienced the story at the bottom. In a glance, you can see that at the top there are just a few marks on the chart, but as you come down the line the marks increase.

What you can expect to see over time is a gradual increase in responses and reactions and then a relatively quick drop off.

What is happening is that at first the person is orientating themselves to the story, getting used to this new sensory adventure. Once orientated they are able to explore it more, and this is where you see the marks on the chart increase and go up. They will hit a point where they are getting maximum enjoyment out of the story, so the marks will be high and many. And then, like all of us, it will start to lose its charm and begin to become boring. At this point, you see the marks on your chart reduce and drop. In the example below showing five charts (Figures 9.1–9.3), you can see that the fourth chart is the peak of engagement and that in the fifth chart, responses have started to drop off. This is when you look for the next sensory story!

This is such a quick and simple system but it has many uses. Handing the chart to someone else and asking them to fill it in can draw awareness to what is happening. Sometimes, watchers of sensory stories can question why a story is being repeated (and may even complain of boredom themselves), but by asking them to fill in the chart you draw them in to what is happening, and when they actively witness that increase in engagement they will realize that although the story is the same, what is happening is not. You'll ignite their excitement.

You can use the charts to explore particular responses – perhaps you are encouraging someone to vocalize more. You could use a little V to indicate a vocalizing response, and an X to indicate other responses; in this way, you could gain extra information about what encourages them to vocalize and use this to plan new experiences for them that give them cause to use their voice.

You could use a similar chart to map out basic sensory preferences; this time the X axis would be divided into types of sensation, for example one column for visual experiences, one for olfactory, one for tactile, and so on. You would make a mark against the type of experience when you saw a response or reaction from your story experiencer. If at the end of the day you have oodles of marks in the olfactory column but none at all in the tactile column then you've heard a clear message from that person as to what sort of sensation they most enjoy. Recording like this can be a way of listening to the opinions and preferences of people who do not use words to communicate.

PART IV

THE SENSORY STORIES AND ASSOCIATED ACTIVITIES

Chapter 10

ABOUT THE SENSORY STORIES AND ASSOCIATED ACTIVITIES

This part of the book contains ten sensory stories, each with activity ideas that could further engagement with the stories. These stories are a sampling of the broad library of sensory stories that are available in the world. Here you will find love stories and life stories, science fiction and science fact, practical stories and silly stories, folklore and fantasy and much more. You can also go online at https://library.jkp.com/redeem and use the voucher code JZWMENS where you will find some little films from me giving extra insight into sensory story creation, and a resource bank of lesson plans relating to the sensory stories authored by me.

For even more stories, visit www.thesensoryprojects.co.uk.

Five of the following stories are authored by me, and five are from amazing guest authors to whom I am gratefully indebted.

The sensory stories and associated resources are presented in the following way:

THE STORY

- *Story text:* The text of the story is presented in a manner that should make it easy for you to photocopy and use. (The pages which can be photocopied are marked with a ✳.)

- *About the story:* An explanation of the story, providing more background information to enable you to tell it in a meaningful way.

RESOURCING THE STORY

- *Shopping list:* A basic list of what you will need for sharing the sensory story, ideal for copying down and creating a shopping list.

- *Detailed list:* A detailed account of each of the stimuli you will need, giving you extra information that will help inform your choices as you select stimuli for your story.

FACILITATING THE STIMULI

- Guidance about how to facilitate the sensory stimuli.

ACTIVITIES

- *Exploration:* Ideas for exploration, often sensory, which can develop a person's connection with, or understanding of, the story.

- *Creative:* Creative ways of engaging with the topics presented within the story.

- *Discovery:* Ways to build learning using the story as a starting point.

The Selkie Wife

When the moon is bright and full
Selkies swim to shore

To shed their skins and dance.

A man once spied the Selkies dancing and wanted one to be his wife. He stole a discarded Selkie skin and locked it in a box.

At dawn their dancing was done, the Selkies dived back into the waves and were gone.

One Selkie could not find her skin, she wept as her friends left without her.

The man comforted the crying Selkie and asked her to be his wife.

The Selkie was happy being married to the man, but at night the smell of the ocean floated through her open window and she longed to be with her friends.

Many years later the Selkie found the box with her skin inside, without a second thought she slipped it on and swam away to dance on distant shores with her friends.

ABOUT THE STORY

This is an old story. It has been told many times in many different ways. Tales of mysterious women are common to mariners. I grew up on a boat and remember my father pointing out seals to our crew, suggesting they might be beautiful women basking on the rocks. Selkies are found in Scottish folklore and by other names in other seafaring lands. In some versions of the story, the man does not know his wife is a Selkie. In others, the Selkie gives birth to a child and the decision to leave for the sea again is made all the harder. In some, the Selkie rescues the man from drowning. However, in all the stories, the Selkie faces the choice of having legs and walking on the land or having a tail and swimming in the sea.

Woven into the few sentences of the story are some lovely messages to share with story experiencers.

- The man watches the Selkies who move in a way that is different from the way he moves, and he sees that movement as beautiful. Many of us move in different ways – some might have limited movements, some jerky movements or twitches, or some might be on wheels. The man saw difference as beautiful. We can all find beautiful ways to move.

- The Selkie, in this story unwillingly but in other stories willingly, gives up her true identity to be with the man. She is able to be happy living on land for a while, but in the end she has to go back to being a Selkie – to being her true self. We may be able to change to suit the needs and desires of others for a while – we may even be able to do so with a smile on our faces – but in the long run each one of us needs to find our own way to be ourselves and express ourselves that makes us joyful, just as the Selkie expresses herself by dancing with her friends.

RESOURCING THE STORY
Shopping list

- Silver tights/stockings

- LED lamp

- White tracing paper/tissue paper

- Music

- A box

- A pipette or a drinking straw

Optional

- A toy tambourine and some coloured ribbons

- Wet rags or pebbles

- Access to the internet or a CD of the 'Wedding March'

Detailed list
Prior to beginning the story:

Sight and touch
A pair of silvery tights: the tights are going to represent the skin of a fish so look for something that will look slippery and silvery like a fish's tail. Cut the tights in half so that each leg is separate, or buy stockings!

When the moon is bright and full

Sight
A round white light source: LED lamps are ideally suited to this, or a torch would work. You can choose to make your light source more moonlike by cutting out a disc of white tracing paper or tissue paper and attaching this to the front of the light source.

Selkies swim to shore

Touch
A washing-up bowl or a water tray filled with cool (but not too cold) water.

> *To shed their skins and dance.*

Touch and sound

Music: a Celtic jig would be appropriate music for Selkies to dance to; alternatively, you can personalize this story to your particular Selkie story experiencer and choose music that will make them want to dance.

You can accentuate the music by providing a hoop with ribbons and bells attached to it for the story experiencer to wave as they dance. If you cannot find one of these you could tie a few coloured ribbons onto the edge of a toy tambourine.

> *A man once spied the Selkies dancing and*
> *wanted one to be his wife. He stole a*
> *discarded Selkie skin and locked it in a box.*

Touch and sight

Find a sturdy box. This is the box that the man will keep the Selkie's skin hidden in for years, so if you are able to find a box with a lock, or paint the inside of the box so that it looks dark and mysterious, this will add to the experience of the story.

> *At dawn their dancing was done, the Selkies*
> *dived back into the waves and were gone.*

Sound

You can make the splashing noises you will need by simply slapping the water in the washing-up bowl with your palm; alternatively drop a succession of objects into the water – wet balls of fabric or pebbles are ideal.

> *One Selkie could not find her skin, she wept as*
> *her friends left without her.*

Touch

You can buy cheap small pipettes online; you might also find them in hardware stores or in pharmacies. If you cannot find a pipette, you can use a drinking straw instead. To use a drinking straw, submerge one end of the straw half a centimeter in water and place your finger over the other end of the straw. When you lift the straw out of the water you will have a drip of water trapped inside the end. To release this water droplet onto the face of the story experiencer, remove your finger from the end of the straw.

> *The man comforted the crying Selkie and*
> *asked her to be his wife.*

Touch and sound

Delivering the comforting touch experience needs no resource other than you. To represent the happy occasion of marriage you can play a peal of church bells – as this is difficult to buy, I recommend looking for something suitable online on YouTube or SoundCloud. An alternative would be to play the 'Wedding March', which you may be able to find in different formats in music shops.

> *The Selkie was happy being married to the*
> *man, but at night the smell of the ocean*
> *floated through an open window and she*
> *longed to be with her friends.*

Smell and touch

Keep your chosen sea smell sealed in a plastic container; by doing this you will allow the air inside the container to become fragranced, thus amplifying the experience of the smell. There are a number of ways you could create the smell of the sea: you can buy essential oils that are meant to represent the smell of the ocean – a few drops of one of these on a cotton pad would work; alternatively, a little bit of fish or seaweed would give off an appropriate odour.

> *Many years later the Selkie found the box*
> *with her skin inside, without a second*
> *thought she slipped it on and swam*
> *away to dance on distant shores with*
> *her friends.*

Touch, sight and sound

No new resources are needed for this final sentence.

FACILITATING THE STIMULI

Prior to beginning the story:
Help the story experiencer to pull the legs of the tights over their hands and arms. This can be done as you announce the name of the story. Seeing the silvery tights and being helped to put them on can act as a sensory cue for the story that is about to be shared.

When the moon is bright and full

Hold the light representing the moon steadily within the gaze of the story experiencer. If you are looking to encourage tracking you can allow the moon to rise during the sentence: hold it with your arm outstretched and parallel to the floor and gradually raise it upwards, keeping your arm straight as you do so, to mimic the curved transit of the moon across the sky (to lift it straight up would make it look as if the moon arrived at its zenith in a lift).

Selkies swim to shore

Support the story experiencer in plunging their arms (clad in tights) into the water. Once submerged, the story experiencer can make a doggy paddle or breaststroke motion.

To shed their skins and dance.

Peel the wet tights off the story experiencer's arms as the music begins to play. You can give the story experiencer a hoop with ribbons and bells tied to it so that they can join in the dancing.

*A man once spied the Selkies dancing and
wanted one to be his wife. He stole a
discarded Selkie skin and locked it in a box.*

Support the story experiencer in picking up the wet tights and dropping them into the box. Close the lid on the box and, if it has a lock, lock it up.

*At dawn their dancing was done, the Selkies
dived back into the waves and were gone.*

Create a series of splashing sounds to represent the Selkies diving into the water. You can do this by slapping the water with your hand or by dropping a series of objects into the water.

> *One Selkie could not find her skin, she wept as*
> *her friends left without her.*

Use the pipette to drip tears onto the face of the story experiencer. Make sure you are using a clean pipette or straw and clean water. Aim for the skin of the cheek near the nose – along the path a tear would follow were it to fall from a crying eye.

> *The man comforted the crying Selkie and*
> *asked her to be his wife.*

If it is appropriate for you to do so, you may hug the story experiencer in a comforting way. Other comforting gestures might be more appropriate, for example laying a hand over the story experiencer's hand or clasping their shoulder. If you are able to provide a peal of wedding bells, these can ring out as the sentence ends.

> *The Selkie was happy being married to the*
> *man, but at night the smell of the ocean*
> *floated through an open window and she*
> *longed to be with her friends.*

Hold the smell to the side of the story experiencer just out of their vision, and use a small fan or sheet of paper to gently waft the scent towards them. Be sure to waft gently otherwise you may just blow the smell past the story experiencer without giving them the time to fully appreciate it.

> *Many years later the Selkie found the box*
> *with her skin inside, without a second*
> *thought she slipped it on and swam*
> *away to dance on distant shores with*
> *her friends.*

There are many ways to facilitate the final sentence of this story in a sensory way; you might choose the one most appropriate to the story experiencer or opt to do several.

- You can grab the wet skin from inside the box.

- You can pull the wet fabric back onto your arms.

- You can 'swim' again in the washing-up bowl or water tray.

- You can play the music that played during the dancing earlier – very quietly at first, as though far away, and gradually getting louder.

EXPLORATION ACTIVITY
Sensory seaside

Create a sensory exploration tray that represents the seaside where the Selkies danced. Consider including shells and pebbles, sand, seaweed, water, and so on. You can play dancing music as you explore the different experiences in the tray.

Separating the items into different bowls can allow you to explore the different sensory aspects of this story in a small space, for example on a lap tray. If you cannot go to the seaside to collect a bowl of seaweed, try using salted spaghetti strands instead – if you cook the spaghetti in water with a few drops of green food colouring then you can create a seaweed-coloured touch experience.

You can freeze your seaside ingredients in a tub of water and then present them either as a block of ice, or smash the ice with a hammer and present them among the slush to be explored.

CREATIVE ACTIVITIES
Movement

You can explore movement by finding different ways to move your body; you can also explore movement by being interested in how others move and finding out how it feels to move in that way by mimicking their movements. Here are some ideas for how to do this.

If I was...places

The Selkies in the story move differently depending on where they are – in the water they swim and on land they dance.

Find images of different places (or sounds from different places) and use these as prompts for your movement. Here are some examples:

- Desert sand: how would you move through deep, slippery desert sand?

- The calm sea: how would you move through a calm sea – would you move in such a way as to try not to disturb it?

- A rough sea: how would your body respond to being buffeted by the waves?

- Hot volcanic rock: how would you move across a hot surface?

- Space: how would you move in an environment with no gravity?

Once you are good at making up lots of different movements you can perform them in a sequence to create a modern dance piece. You could add music and sounds relevant to the places to your dance.

If I was...animals

Animals move in lots of different ways.

Use images of animals, or the sounds made by animals, as prompts for movement. Here are some examples:

- A hummingbird: can you move so fast that your limbs are a blur?

- A snake: can you move without using your arms or legs?

- A panther: can you move in a slinky, sleek way?

- A cormorant: can you bob about almost still and then suddenly dive and glide?

You can develop this activity by looking at the life cycle of a particular animal and creating movements to suit all the stages of its life. These movements can be performed in sequence to create a dance piece.

If I was...imagination

Invent rules for the ways your body can move. Here are some examples:

- If my elbows were made of jelly I would move like this...

- If I had two arms growing out of my head, but none on my body, I would move like this...

- If my feet were made of ice, I would move like this...

- If the floor were very sticky, I would move like this...

- If my body did not bend, I would move like this...

If I was...you

For this version of 'If I was' you need to be in a group of friends. If you have not got a group you can explore movement with, you might be able to use the internet to get ideas for people who move in different ways.

Take it in turns to copy the movement of your friends. You are not doing this to make fun of their movement but to find out what it feels like to move as they do.

If your friends have particular skills that they can perform – for example, martial arts, dance or swimming – perhaps they can teach you some of the movements from those things. If your friends have limitations on their movements, taking time to understand how this feels physically can help you to feel closer to them. Remember, everyone can move in a way that is beautiful – by exploring each other's movements you can discover new ways of being beautiful.

Sequencing movements

With all of the 'If I was' games there are opportunities to sequence the movements. Sequencing and rehearsing a sequence of movements is not only good for the body, but can also help to improve the memory. You can create a sequence in the same way as you would play a memory game such as, 'I went to the shops and I bought...' Try an imaginary journey on which you see a lot of animals, for example:

- Person 1: 'I went on an adventure and I saw a hummingbird' – flap arms very fast.

- Person 2: 'I went on an adventure and I saw a snake' – slither on the floor, 'and a hummingbird' – flap arms very fast.

- Person 3: 'I went on an adventure and I saw a dolphin' – jump and then undulate your body as if swimming butterfly stroke, 'and a snake' – slither on the floor, 'and a hummingbird' – flap arms very fast. And so on.

Performing the movements will make it easier to remember the animals encountered on the adventure.

You can create a sequence of movements to tell the Selkie story. Invent your own or use the suggestions below.

When the moon is bright and full

Begin curled up in a tight ball on the floor, uncurl and stretch your arms wide and open to be the bright fullness of the moon.

> *Selkies swim to shore*

Move around the space as if swimming.

> *To shed their skins and dance.*

Imagine you are peeling yourself out of your skin – begin at your ribs and roll your imagined skin all the way down to your toes, step out of it and dance.

> *A man once spied the Selkies dancing and*
> *wanted one to be his wife.*
> *He stole a discarded Selkie skin and*
> *locked it in a box.*

Creep about as if sneaking through the dance to steal the skin.

> *At dawn their dancing was done, the Selkies*
> *dived back into the waves and were gone.*

Dance, look up suddenly as if spotting the rising sun, leap as if diving into water, and then move in swimming movements again.

> *One Selkie could not find her skin, she wept*
> *as her friends left without her.*

Imagine you are the one Selkie left behind on the beach – run frantically from side to side, stop and swing your arms around as if asking anyone where your skin could be, before falling to your knees and hiding your eyes as if crying.

> *The man comforted the crying Selkie and*
> *asked her to be his wife.*

If you are doing these movements with a friend, one of you can play the part of the man and comfort the Selkie on her knees. If you are performing alone, you can join this section of the story to the next section.

> *The Selkie was happy being married to the*
> *man, but at night the smell of the ocean*
> *floated through her open window and she*
> *longed to be with her friends.*

Move as if doing household chores and look happy. Lie down as if to sleep but toss and turn restlessly, and then get up to lean out of a window. Imagine yourself carried away in your movements by moving around the space, rising and falling as if carried away by waves.

> *Many years later the Selkie found the box*
> *with her skin inside, without a second*
> *thought she slipped it on and swam*
> *away to dance on distant shores with*
> *her friends.*

Mime opening a box and look surprised. Roll your skin on from your toes to your ribs and then leap and swim and dance jubilantly.

If you are performing this movement sequence with friends, you can each take different roles and turn the dance into a play.

DISCOVERY ACTIVITIES
Losing, hiding and finding
One of the themes of this story is loss. We have all had experiences of losing things, some of them big, some of them small.

Finding
Playing games that involve searching for lost things can be a lot of fun. In the sensory story the Selkie's lost skin is represented by a pair of silvery tights. You could play hide and seek with the tights. One person pretends to be the man and the other the Selkie. While the Selkie is not looking, the man hides her skin (the tights) somewhere in the room. It is then the Selkie's job to find the tights.

Hiding
Object permanence – knowing that an object is still there when we cannot see it anymore – is part of the development of our understanding. Hiding an object in a box that the story experiencer can see and then allowing them to open the box

and find the object reinforces object permanence. Exploring boxes to find out what is inside can be a fun extension of this – use shredded paper or packing material to fill the box and then hide different things inside. You can choose things that provide a variety of sensory stimulation – try a lemon or orange with the rind removed for an interesting-to-touch, smelly object, sunglasses for a discoverable sight experience or a rattle or bell for a sound experience.

For more able story experiencers create personalized boxes in which to hide treasured possessions. Once you have got a box with treasure in, it is only natural to draw a treasure map to remind you of its hiding place. You can make a game for two players based on the battleships game, out of hidden treasure and maps. Here's how to do it.

Hidden treasure
Preparation

- Each player draws a grid eight squares wide and eight squares high.

- Label the squares along one axis with letters and the squares along the other axis with numbers. At this point both players' maps look the same.

- Each player has four boxes of treasure that they can hide anywhere on their map.

- Players must hide their maps from each other and not peek at each other's.

- One treasure box is very big; it is three squares wide and three squares high. One treasure box is very small, it is just one square. The remaining boxes are medium sized; each one is two squares by two squares.

- Players can, just for fun, draw other details on their grids to make them look more map-like.

Playing the game

- Once each player has hidden their treasure on their map the hunting can begin. Take it in turns to hunt for treasure by calling out a grid reference, for example, B3.

- When one player calls out a grid reference the other player must look in that square and reply 'Treasure' if there is treasure in that square or 'Keep hunting' if there is not.

- The player who called out the grid reference can make a mark on their map to remember which squares they have asked about – writing T in squares where treasure has been found and X in squares where there was no treasure can help them to keep track of their search.

- The player who uncovers all of the other player's treasure first is the winner.

You can change the game by making your starting grid bigger or smaller and having more or less treasure. A big grid with a little treasure in will be very hard; a small grid with a lot of treasure will be very easy.

You can extend this game by requiring answering players to say how many squares away from treasure a certain square is. For example, if player one calls B3 and player two has no treasure in B3, but does have treasure buried four squares away they would respond 'four'.

The story below can be sung to the tune of The Searchers' song 'Sugar and Spice'.

Seasoned with Spice
Season with spice and all things nice,
Together we will spend this time,
Season with spice and all things nice,
You know our dinner will taste fine.

We all work together to cook our
Dinner in this family.

Be careful 'cause the pots and pans are hot
As they sit upon the stove. You know it is

Seasoned with spice and all things nice,
Together we will spend this time.

Seasoned with spice and all things nice,
You know our dinner will taste fine.

The cutlery clatters as we pass the
Plates around the table.

We chatter and smile as we share our food,
Sitting altogether here. You know it is

Seasoned with spice and all things nice,
Together we will spend this time.

Seasoned with spice and all things nice,
You know our dinner will taste fine.

Everyone around this table loves me,
This is my family.

Sharing food together is a pleasure,
Friendship, laughs and company. You know it is

Seasoned with spice and all things nice,
Together we spent this time.

Seasoned with spice and all things nice,
You know our dinner tasted fine.

ABOUT THE STORY

Cooking is a very sensory-rich experience – aside from the tastes and smells of food, there are all the sounds of kitchen implements clattering, whisking, blending and boiling, together with the chatter of the family as they ready themselves for sharing a meal. All sensory experiences are valuable, especially to people with profound and multiple learning disabilities, and finding ways to include people with particular needs in those experiences is worth doing. A story like this, which introduces cooking, could be told in the kitchen, accustoming the story experiencer to everything that goes on in there so that they could join in. Perhaps you could even improvise your own songs around things you cook.

John Ockenden, Practice Development Advisor for United Response (2006), studied how staff in care homes engaged adults with profound and multiple learning disabilities in activities. Ockenden comments that, 'too many adults with profound and multiple learning disabilities are sitting around with nothing to do, just because it is not immediately obvious either that they want to be engaged, or how to enable them to be' (2006, p.7). One area he identified in particular was cooking; he noted that when there was cooking to be done, the adults with profound and multiple learning disa-bilities tended to be left in a different room so that staff members could get on with the task in hand. The staff missed out on an opportunity to provide their clients with the richly stimulating sensory experience. You can use this sensory story/song to introduce cooking to the story experiencer. Because cooking is such a richly stimulating experience, and kitchens themselves can also be rich experiences, some people may initially find them overwhelming. By sharing this story in a neutral setting, you can build up to sharing it in the kitchen and allowing the story experiencer to become accustomed to everything that is in the kitchen. I hope that in the future you will be able to share cooking as well as stories and songs.

This story/song has been written specifically with blind people in mind. It provides rich opportunities to interact via touch, taste and smell. The single visual experience in the story can easily be replaced, for example with recordings of different people's voices or with objects to touch that represent the different people around the table.

Singing is a very powerful force when it comes to memory. I expect that, no matter how old you are, you will be able to remember a song you sang at school. Singing is great for encouraging people to join in with sound making or vocalization; it does not matter if you cannot pronounce the words, you can still join in. Even those without a voice at all can join in with singing by playing along on musical instruments. Sharing a song unites a group and helps everyone to feel included. The repeating verse will further support those who want to join in but struggle to do so completely.

Try repeating each verse by humming it gently before proceeding to the next verse; this will support the telling of the story in a number of ways.

- Humming will help you not to waffle while the story experiencer is interacting with the stimuli. (See Chapter 3 for the importance of this.)

- Alternating between singing and humming will provide a rhythm to the experience of the story, which will help the story experiencer know what to expect. As you sing, they can join in with singing and vocalizing. As you hum, they can explore the stimuli.

- Humming the entire verse before proceeding to the next one will support you in allowing the story experiencer enough time to fully explore the stimuli. It can be tempting to move on quickly from a stimulus, especially a smell. If you remove a stimulus too quickly, the story experiencer may not have time to fully process the experience; keeping a stimulus present for the duration of a verse gives the story experiencer a decent amount of time to interact with it, and you can always hum the verse again if you feel they need more time.

RESOURCING THE STORY
Shopping list

- Fragrant spices (or herbs) – be sure to choose ones that are safe for the story experiencer

- Saucepan

- Cutlery and plates

- Photographs of family members (or objects of reference that relate to them)

Optional

- Rice or couscous, cooking apples or chopped tomatoes

Detailed list

Season with spice and all things nice,
Together we will spend this time,
Season with spice and all things nice,
You know our dinner will taste fine.

Smell, taste and touch

Fragrant spices (or herbs): try to choose spices with a distinctive smell. Be aware that some spices in large quantities can be poisonous or cause skin or eye irritations. Also be aware of any allergies the story experiencer may have. Instead of presenting the story experiencer with just the raw spices, you can use them to fragrance something else (see below for ideas). Doing this can be a good way of getting the smell and taste benefits of the spices without risking exposure to too great a quantity of them. Also, having a spiced foodstuff can make it easier for the story experiencer to be able to touch the stimuli. Cooking actions like stirring or rubbing can accentuate the smell experience and are appropriate for these sections of the story.

This stimulus is repeated four times over the course of the sensory song. You may want to encourage the story experiencer to move from smelling, to smelling and touching, to smelling and touching around the face, through to smelling and tasting as the song progresses.

Ideas for spiced dishes:

- Cook rice with a little coriander.

- Cook couscous in butter with a little garlic.

- Heat some chopped tomatoes with a little curry powder.

- Stew apples with a little allspice or nutmeg.

- Cook a spiced dish you know or use a shop-bought curry sauce to coat potatoes or rice.

You could also make sweets with spices in. Here is a simple recipe for fudge which you can add spices to – try the following combinations:

- White chocolate with vanilla essence.

- Dark chocolate with ginger or cinnamon.

- Milk chocolate with raisins and nutmeg.

To make the fudge, simply melt 500g of chocolate slowly in a pan, with 400g of condensed milk and 75g of unsalted butter. When the chocolate and the butter have melted, stir in your choice of spices. Pour the mixture into a greased tray and leave in the fridge to cool; you can then cut it into squares and taste it.

When considering food stimuli, decide whether a dry option such as rice or couscous is more suitable to the story experiencer than a wet option such as chopped tomatoes or stewed apples. The wet options might make for a more pleasant taste experience but be off-putting to someone who finds getting their fingers sticky difficult. Consider also whether sweet or savoury will be more appropriate and which will be most likely to engage your audience. Of course, you can opt to have a different experience for each repeat of the 'Seasoned with spice' section – you could imagine that there were different components to the dish, and fudge for dessert.

We all work together to cook our
Dinner in this family.

Be careful 'cause the pots and pans are hot
As they sit upon the stove. You know it is

Touch

Saucepan: any pot or pan you have around the house will do. Obviously, you are not going to present the story experiencer with a pan that is hot from the stove. Warming up the pan by standing it on a hot water bottle, or running it under the hot tap, can give a relevant touch experience of warm metal without being dangerous.

Seasoned with spice and all things nice…

Smell, taste and touch
As with verse I.

*The cutlery clatters as we pass the
Plates around the table.*

*We chatter and smile as we share our food,
Sitting altogether here. You know it is*

Sound and touch
Cutlery and plates: choose a combination that will clatter well – metal knives and forks on plastic plates is a good one.

Seasoned with spice and all things nice…

Smell, taste and touch
As with verse I.

*Everyone around this table loves me,
This is my family.*

*Sharing food together is a pleasure,
Friendship, laughs and company. You know it is*

Sight
Photographs of family members: you can interpret the word 'family' to include all those who care for us as if they were family, so including pictures of friends is appropriate. If you are able to laminate the images they will last longer. If you want to create the feeling of these beloved people being all around, try hanging the images from a curve of cardboard or a bent metal coat hanger so that they can dangle in a semicircle around the story experiencer. Be mindful of where they will be best placed to enable the story experiencer to see them – some experiencers will need to view them closer than others.

Seasoned with spice and all things nice…

Smell, taste and touch
As with verse 1.

FACILITATING THE STIMULI

> *Season with spice and all things nice,*
> *Together we will spend this time.*
>
> *Season with spice and all things nice,*
> *You know our dinner will taste fine.*

Offer the story experiencer the spices or spiced rice/couscous mix to smell. Think about how you will present this stimulus – you may choose to use a mixing bowl or something similar that is linked to cooking. Choosing a relatively deep bowl will make it easy for the story experiencer to interact with the stimuli without spilling it. Alternatively, having the stimuli stored in a sealed plastic pot will allow for the air inside the pot to become fragranced and so present a stronger stimulus when opened.

This stimulus repeats four times through the sensory song. You can encourage greater interaction with it on each successive experience. First, the story experiencer may just be sniffing the stimulus; they can then move on to touching it – disturbing the mix may well increase the smell; if it is safe to do so, they can also be encouraged to taste it.

If you have made a spiced rice or couscous mix then presenting it warm is another way of increasing the impact of the smell. If you have made fudge you could present it before it is set, then you would have a fragrant gloopy substance to explore.

> *We all work together to cook our*
> *Dinner in this family.*
>
> *Be careful 'cause the pots and pans are hot*
> *As they sit upon the stove. You know it is*

Pass the story experiencer a warm pan. Support them in exploring the feeling of the warm metal. Note: Do not use a pan hot from the stove (see the guidance in the detailed shopping list for advice on how to heat the pan safely).

> *Seasoned with spice and all things nice...*

As with verse 1.

> *The cutlery clatters as we pass the*
> *Plates around the table.*
>
> *We chatter and smile as we share our food,*
> *Sitting altogether here. You know it is*

As long as you have chosen cutlery and plates that will clatter nicely, this stimulus is easy to facilitate. Simply pass the cutlery and plates between you. It does not matter if they get dropped – that will just cause more clattering.

> *Seasoned with spice and all things nice...*

As with verse 1.

> *Everyone around this table loves me,*
> *This is my family.*
>
> *Sharing food together is a pleasure,*
> *Friendship, laughs and company. You know it is*

Display the images of family and friends at a distance at which the story experiencer will be able to see them easily. If the story experiencer finds a multitude of images difficult to focus on, try presenting them one by one or moving them steadily across their vision.

> *Seasoned with spice and all things nice...*

As with verse 1.

> *Seasoned with spice and all things nice,*
> *Together we spent this time.*
>
> *Seasoned with spice and all things nice,*
> *You know our dinner tasted fine.*

EXPLORATION ACTIVITIES
Tactile kitchen

Explore how things in the kitchen feel. If you are supporting a deafblind story experiencer you can help them locate items by gently using a hand-under-hand technique to guide them to cupboard doors, drawers, etc.

If you think about a kitchen as a tactile environment, you will very quickly realize what a rich set of sensory experiences it holds: the coldness of metal; the warmth of wooden chopping boards; the stippled nature of plastic chopping boards, graters and even sieves; the grooves in colanders; the shapes of handles, spoons and taps; the wetness of water; the warmth of the oven (be careful of course).

You can add structure to this activity by sorting the different experiences. You can sort kitchen items according to their material: wood, plastic, glass and ceramics. You can create an order of experiences, for example from bumpy to smooth, or from warm to cool.

Musical kitchen

As anyone who has ever banged a wooden spoon on an upturned saucepan knows, the kitchen is a wonderful source of musical instruments. Rhythm is a very important part of language acquisition, so despite what it may do to your ears, allowing a person to bang on an improvised drum can be beneficial to their development. If you also bang on something then you can help them to keep the beat.

It does not just have to be drums; exploring the different sounds in the kitchen can be a fascinating experience. These are noises that you probably hear every day and consequently pay little attention to, but if you stop and concentrate on them you can discover a rich auditory environment. Think about: the rattle of cutlery as the drawer is opened; the shiver of a whisk banged against the palm; the squeak of a glass as you rub a damp finger around its rim; the different sounds made by the different materials – making drums of different materials and using different materials as drumsticks; the pops and slurping sounds of lids being removed; the sound of things being cut with knives – vegetables, bread and cheese; the sound of tin foil being torn off a roll; the sound of a tin opener gradually nibbling its way through metal.

To add structure to your sound explorations you can try to create a tune. Filling mugs with different amounts of water and hitting them with a teaspoon can give you melodic notes to accompany your strong rhythm section. If you do not feel you have the musical ability to master a tune, try sound matching activities; for example, what sounds as squeaky as a mouse? What sound is quiet enough to go unnoticed in a library? What sound is as loud as an elephant? Once you have got the hang of this, you can begin to create marvellous soundscapes.

A soundscape is not a tune, nor is it a full narrative, but it can tell a story. Think of the way a picture can tell a story. A soundscape is the auditory equivalent of a picture. You could create an eerie soundscape by having shivery sounds (tin foil shaking gently or a hand whisk turning slowly) gradually building up, with a sudden *bang!* at the end. You could create a magical soundscape by having lots of melodic plinking sounds (spoons hitting bottles filled with water, jars of preserves or just against each other) followed by a warm whooshing sound (the sound of the fan oven being turned on) or a happy *ping!* (as the microwave finishes its cycle). Thinking about how the sounds make you feel and deciding whether they are happy or sad sounds can help inform your choices for soundscapes. If you enjoy this activity you could try and build bespoke soundscapes, perhaps using stories or pictures for inspiration: if someone sends you a postcard, can you create a soundscape that suits it? Can you think of a soundscape that would introduce a play of your favourite story? Noticing how sounds are used in TV programmes and films to add interest can help you to hone your soundscaping skills.

Colour and texture exploration

The kitchen can be an artist's playground with so many natural colours and textures available to make a collage with. Exploring food in a playful way can help children who are reluctant eaters to feel relaxed around it, and, as long as you are using food that does not need cooking, if it happens to get on the fingers and into the mouth while you are being creative, it does not matter, is not a big deal and can be a very casual way to introduce new flavours and textures to a sensitive palate.

Here are some creative ideas to get you started.

- *Foods as paints:* Get a cupcake tray and fill each with a different food substance from the kitchen. Take a paintbrush and a sheet of sugar paper (sugar paper is a good choice as it is very absorbent, but any sort of paper will do) and get painting. You may find diluting some foods makes them easier to paint with. If you want the story experiencer to experience the textures of the foods without them being diluted then by using a piece of stiff card and a pallet knife, you can show them how the great oil painters of old often applied their paint to their canvas with a knife.

- *Fruit and vegetable portraits:* Have a look at the work of Giuseppe Arcimboldo for inspiration and see if you can set out fruit and vegetables to look like a human face. Having a soft base to place the fruit and vegetables onto will help you to create your portrait. A section of duvet or a bed of scrunched up newspaper will both provide soft bases and stop your creations from rolling away.

- *Face plates:* Make your lunch look like a face. There are so many different ways to do this and you can have fun creating your own ideas. Here are a few to get you started:

  - Eyes: Raisins, grapes, small cheese crackers, marshmallows, pepperoni slices.

  - Noses: Slices of cheese, triangular sandwiches, a carrot with its base cut off sticking straight up off the plate.

  - Mouths: Red pepper slices, rolled ham, a sprinkled curve of fine grains: a rice mixture, couscous, nuts and seeds, half a round cracker spread with jam.

  Think also of how you might create: cheeks, freckles, moustaches, eyebrows, chins, ears, facial jewellery!

- *Mashed potato landscapes:* Using mashed potato as a base for culinary art can be a very versatile approach. You can sculpt the potato into hills and slopes and add broccoli trees and little huts made of vegetable sticks. Colour the potato with streaks of ketchup or blended peas. Create mosaics with sliced vegetables. Let your imagination run riot.

CREATIVE ACTIVITIES
Family boxes
Create treasure boxes full of information about your family and friends.

Preparation
You will need some boxes – shoeboxes are ideal and if you ask in shoe shops they often have spare boxes.

Label the lid of each box with a photograph of a family member. You can label them with a tactile reference, if photos are not useful to you. Wrapping the boxes in different colours of wrapping paper can help to distinguish them – you could get the person in the photograph to choose their favourite wrapping paper from a selection or you could ask them their favourite colour and then wrap the box accordingly.

Activity

This is an activity to be done over time. If you are supporting someone in creating these boxes it can be nice to put a few things in each box to get them started.

Fill the boxes with things that relate to the person pictured on their lids. Here are some ideas:

- A dab of their perfume or deodorant on a cotton pad sealed in a plastic pot, for a smell of them.

- A piece of fabric or an old piece of their clothing washed in their usual laundry detergent.

- Some of their favourite snacks.

- A lock of hair.

- A sample bottle of their favourite shampoo, soap, shower gel or moisturiser.

- Photos that relate to the person.

- Items that represent activities you share together, for example books, balls, pieces from board games.

You can use the boxes as memory boxes and keep things like letters and cards in them, as well as photographs. You could write about activities you have shared together and keep the accounts in the box to come back to at a later date. You might want to find out the same information about everyone, and keep a record. Making an old-fashioned set of sorting cards can be a fun way to do this.

Cooking

There are so many things you can cook using herbs and spices. There is a yummy recipe for fudge in the detailed shopping list, and there are many recipes that have herbs and spices among their ingredients.

Thinking of cooking as a sensory experience can open you up to creating your own dishes and becoming an intuitive cook. Below is an easy savoury recipe that you can adapt to use various herbs and spices. Have fun exploring different flavour combinations.

You will need

- A large wok

- A wooden spoon

Ingredients

- A dash of olive oil

- A selection of vegetables – try to choose lots of different colours; it will be a healthier meal and look more interesting

- A tin of chopped tomatoes

- Whatever herbs and spices you fancy

Method

- Chop the vegetables into thin strips – pieces the length of your little finger and the width of a pencil are perfect.

- Add a dash of oil to the wok and place it on a hot stove.

- Add the vegetables and keep stirring so they do not stick to the bottom. If you have chosen to include onions, adding them first can give them lots of time to caramelize, giving a nice sweet taste to the meal. You can choose to add firmer vegetables such as carrots rather than softer vegetables like peppers.

- If you plan on using fresh spices such as ginger or garlic, slice them finely and add them during this stage, along with the vegetables.

- Once the vegetables look nearly cooked (onions will become clear, other vegetables might become floppier or change colour slightly, peppers will brown a little), add the tin of chopped tomatoes. Keep stirring until the tomatoes are warmed through and then add your herbs and spices. Add them a little at a time and keep tasting the mixture to see if it tastes good. Be aware that some flavours will change the more they are cooked.

DISCOVERY ACTIVITIES
Nobody's nose!

(My thanks to the Dayton family for introducing me to this game.)

This is a game you can play to find out how well you know your loved ones. It is fun to play at family events, so if you are having a birthday party or having friends round to dinner or a play date, think about setting up a Nobody's nose board.

Preparation

Find photographs of all your friends and family and enlarge them using a computer or photocopier, then cut out just the noses. Depending on how hard you want to make the game, add in one or a few noses of people who are not among your family and friends; this nose will be the Nobody's nose. Mix all the noses up and stick them on a board. Number the noses and display the board somewhere where everybody will be able to see it.

To play

The aim of the game is to identify which one of the noses on the board is Nobody's nose.

Allow each person a certain amount of time to look at the board; they can then write down their guess on a slip of paper. Once everyone has had the chance to guess you can reveal your guesses and see who has identified Nobody's nose. For a more gentle pace of play, simply display the board with slips of paper next to it and a box to post answers into. People can view the board at their leisure, write their name and their guess on a slip of paper and post it into the box. At a suitable point during the day, someone can open the box and read out the guesses to discover who has identified Nobody's nose.

Extension

For extra points, you can ask people to identify which nose is whose. To help, you can provide a list of the names of people whose noses are on display. You might be able to use a nose of a celebrity or public figure as the Nobody's nose to help everyone with their guessing.

Variations

- *Different body parts:* Try the game using different body parts, what about 'Eye eye!' for identifying whose eyes are pictured? Mouths, eyebrows and even chins can all be interesting parts to identify. If the game is too difficult with just one body part, try pairing them up so that people have a nose and a mouth to go on when they are guessing.

- *Different items:* Try taking photos of people's shoes, coats, scarves, socks or hair, and see if friends and family members can identify each other from these objects.

- *Real items:* Ask everyone attending your party to bring an item with them that they feel represents them. Label each item with a number and play the game in the same way as if you had a board of noses. Alternatively, put all the items into a pillowcase and have the guests at the party pass the pillowcase around and each take out an item. Then go around the circle and have each person guess whose object they are holding. You will need to add in a random item that does not belong to anyone in the room – charity shops are a good source of such items. You can theme the items you ask your guests to bring to the party so that you can play the game again and again. Here are some ideas for things to request:

  - Favourite song

  - Favourite teddy bear

  - Best pair of socks

  - Favourite food

  - Favourite picture (not photograph)

  - A sample of their handwriting – you could ask people to write a particular message relating to the party, for example, 'Happy Birthday, Nina'.

Plaster of paris

If you have adventurous family members and friends you might be able to persuade them to allow you to make plaster of paris models of their body parts. Some body parts are harder to do than others, but hands are an easy place to start.

You will need

- Play-doh

- Plaster of paris

- A tub large enough for people to fit their hands into – a large ice cream tub is ideal (and also a great excuse for having to eat lots of ice cream!)

To make a cast of someone's hand

Half fill the tub with play-doh. Smooth the play-doh out so that it is as level as you can get it. Ask your friend or family member to press their hand firmly into it and then to remove it gently. Check the imprint they have left: does it look like their hand? Have they pressed all their fingers down equally? If it looks okay then it is good to use; if you are not confident then re-smooth the play-doh and ask them to try again.

Mix up some plaster of paris and pour it into the imprint of your friend or family member's hand in the play-doh. Do not worry if it goes over the edges in places – as it is in the tub you will not make a mess.

Leave the plaster hand to set. Once it has gone hard you can lift it out of the tub and clean off any bits of play-doh that have stuck to it.

Sorting cards

Sorting cards can be used to identify a person from a set of simple questions. Creating a deck of sorting cards is a good way to stimulate curiosity about our similarities and differences. You can make sorting cards to use as a reference for any group of people or items – for example, a set of sorting cards based on a toy collection, or on possible holiday destinations, or on the professionals you meet in hospital.

Preparation

You will need a set of cards that are all the same shape – index cards can be perfect for the job but you may want something larger. Pieces of A5 card would be ideal.

Decide what information you want to find out about everyone, for example:

- eye colour

- hair colour

- gender

- are they a family member or a friend?

- do you know them from home or from school?

- are they an adult or a child?

Each item needs to be something that can be phrased as a yes or no question, for example 'eye colour' could be phrased as, 'Do you have brown eyes?'

Take one index card and punch evenly spaced holes in it down two opposite sides using a hole punch. Leave the top left-hand hole blank; beside each of the other holes write one of your questions.

Punch holes in all the other cards in the same place as the first card.

Creating the sorting cards

Take one pre-punched card to interview each family member or friend. Use the card with the questions on as a reference. Write the name of the person who you are interviewing on the new card. If they answer a question with a 'no', cut the hole that relates to that question so that it becomes a notch in the side of the card.

Using the sorting cards

Once you have made all your cards, you can use them to find out which family members have things in common with each other. Stack all the cards so that they line up nicely. Poke a pencil or stick through the hole that has no question associated with it. Choose a question you wish to ask, for example, 'Who has brown eyes?' Push another pencil or stick through the hole that is associated with that question and lift the deck of cards up. All those people who have brown eyes will swing out of the deck and dangle from one pencil only. If you want to ask a combination question, you just need another pencil, for example, you could find out which boys have brown eyes or which people from school have brown eyes.

Grow your own

This activity presents many opportunities for sensory exploration, such as handling compost, pressing compost into pots, handling herbs, smelling herbs, hearing water pouring.

Making your own garden of herbs and spices will bring you the joy and satisfaction of watching plants grow as well as being a fragrant addition to any room. Cooking with herbs and spices you have grown yourself is more rewarding than cooking with ones bought from the shops and may encourage reluctant eaters to try new flavours.

Preparation

Find a large plastic pot with holes in the bottom. If you cannot find a large one you could use several smaller ones. Supermarkets often package fruit and vegetables in plastic pots with holes in the bottom. Stand your pot in a tray on top of several bottle lids. The bottle lids will raise the pot away from the tray a little and allow any excess water to drain out easily. Fill your pots with soil or compost.

Growing your herbs and spices

If you have patience then you can grow plants from seeds. Some seeds will grow more quickly than others – cress is a quick grower.

If you want an instant garden, you could go to a garden centre to pick up some small plants. Supermarkets often sell herbs growing in small pots but these are not intended for replanting and may not last long if you try to grow them.

Remember to keep an eye on your plants and keep the soil damp. Placing the pot somewhere where it will get sunlight will help to keep your plants healthy.

It can be nice to choose herbs that produce a scent when rubbed gently between the fingers, as then you can experience their aroma without having to deprive the plant of its foliage; herbs like lemon balm and rosemary are good for this.

Concerns about playing with your food

We all know that playing with your food is the gravest flouting of table manners there can be. It is natural that we would worry that allowing children to play with food will encourage bad table manners.

There are two things it is important to consider if you are worried about table manners: your priorities and the context.

Your priorities

Playing with food can take away the associated anxiety some children feel about eating. If the story experiencer has difficulties eating, it is likely that it is a higher priority for you that they learn to eat and feel safe and happy doing so, before they learn their table manners. I expect if you had a choice between them having perfect table manners and never being able to eat without experiencing anxiety or being able to eat happily but not doing so in a particularly standard way, you would choose the latter option.

Context

Context plays an enormous role in behaviour. It is possible to teach a person that this sort of behaviour is okay in one situation but not in another. If you are worried that the playing with food behaviour will carry over into mealtimes, avoid doing playful activities at the dinner table.

If you are sharing these activities with someone who avoids eating or becomes distressed around eating, you may want to create a progression that ends up at the dinner table. First, they play with food substances that do not look like food they recognize in a context entirely unrelated to eating. They move along the progression, next playing with food substances that are more recognizable to them as food and in locations more associated with food, until they end up playing with what you hope they will eat for dinner at the dinner table. This can be a very sensible strategy for helping someone to get over their fears surrounding food. If, as soon as you get to the table with real food, you then add in the pressure to behave in a certain way, you inadvertently send messages of anxiety. It is good to allow a period of time where the person is able to play with their food – and eat it – at the dinner table, before you begin to introduce table manners, so the habit of eating at the table has the chance to become established.

Once you have a person eating happily, you can begin to teach table manners. Table manners are very much a matter of context; for example, eating with our fingers at the table would be frowned on whereas eating with our fingers at a picnic might not be. Making the person you are teaching aware of the different contexts is the first step. You can support their awareness of context by clearly labelling each situation. You can do this verbally, encouraging them to use words such as inside, outside, table, garden. You can do this through symbols or objects of reference – reinforce the context by presenting the relevant symbol or object at the right time; for example, handing the person a symbol of the table as they go to the table and having a matching symbol on the table where they can place the symbol they are carrying.

Talking about what we do in different places before entering them can help to prepare a person for the behaviour that will be expected of them once they get there. It also means that any tension that might arise out of the desire to modify behaviour will not be directly associated with the place. You can make this a fun learning game by adding role-play and getting them to copy your actions; for example, present the picture of the table and ask, 'What do we do here?' then answer your own question with actions and encourage the person to join in. Remember to include details that are not related to eating so that it does not become an eating-focused lesson. Things you might do include: say, 'Sit on your bottom,' and then sit down as if on a chair; say, 'Keep your elbows off the table,' and then stick your elbows out to show what elbows are and then pull them back to your ribs; say, 'Use our knife and fork,' and then mime cutting with a knife and lifting food with a fork. You can include things like elbows off the table, as long as joining in feels fun. If this activity is fun then when the person is at the table they will be able to do these movements and the emotion associated with them will be one of joy (not one of being told off).

Difficult tasks like cutting food with a knife can be stressful if they are first encountered alongside being expected to eat a certain quantity of food, so practising these skills through play in other situations can help. Remember that cutting play-doh is much easier than cutting food, as you can just apply pressure to a knife instead of a sawing motion. Try to present lots of opportunities to cut different things and learn how to hold them still with a fork while sawing with a knife. You can contrast table manners with expected behaviour elsewhere. Choose places where you might eat when exploring behaviour like the park, as well as places you would not eat, like the swimming pool, for example.

Two People Made Me

One egg from Mummy and one sperm from
Daddy and there I was! One cell dividing
and growing inside Mummy's womb.

My heart began to beat and my eyes grew,
though I kept them closed.

I grew fingers and toes, I swam and I kicked.
My skin was covered with soft lanugo fur.

As my ears developed I began to hear
sounds from outside the womb.

Mummy ate for me. I could taste bitter and sweet.

The bigger I grew the more squashed I became.
On my birthday Mummy and I worked hard
to bring me into the world.

And then I was here! Able to stretch out, see,
smell, touch, taste and hear: ready to explore the world.

ABOUT THE STORY

Pregnancy can be a mysterious time; from the outside we watch a bump grow. A mother-to-be may feel her baby move; she will feel her body change and grow to support her baby, but what is going on inside the womb is hidden. Developments in science and human understanding can now tell us what is happening inside the womb at every stage of pregnancy: we know when a foetus first opens its mouth and tastes the amniotic waters in which it swims; we know when its fingers and toes form; we know when it begins to hear.

Each one of us was once inside a bump, and knowing about this very early part of our lives can be fascinating. We may have had the experience of watching a bump grow and waiting to meet our child, our sibling or a new friend, and knowing about their development as they grow can help us to get to know them before they are born.

Many people have journeys to pregnancy and birth that are different in some way to the one described here. Change the words of the story to suit your personal journey. For example, you may want to add that doctors and nurses worked hard to bring your child into the world, or you could say Mummy's egg and a sperm if conception was a result of sperm donation. You may also want to adapt the final line of the story to reflect the capabilities your child has; for example, replacing seeing with giggling and resourcing this with a tickle instead of a sight experience. Personalizing the story will make it a more powerful experience for the story experiencer.

RESOURCING THE STORY
Shopping list

- A single ball

- A drum (or sturdy cardboard box)

- Fur fabric or velvet

- A large, cardboard takeaway cup (the perfect excuse to treat yourself to a drink when you are shopping)

- Lemon juice

- Honey

- A large scarf or sheet

- Your choice for multiple sensory stimuli – see detailed list

Detailed list

> *One egg from Mummy and one sperm from*
> *Daddy and there I was! One cell dividing*
> *and growing inside Mummy's womb.*

Touch

Understanding the concept of oneness is actually quite hard to do. Before we are able to count, we need to have had experiences of one and many. The repeated use of the word 'one' in this phrase is a good opportunity to reinforce a link between a single item and the word 'one'. It is useful if you can choose an item that does not already have its own connotations in the mind of the story experiencer; for example, do not use their favourite toy or an item familiar to them by a different name. A single ball would be a simple way of handing the story experiencer an experience of oneness.

You may be able to highlight further the oneness of the item you present to the story experiencer by having many others present; for example, lifting one marble from a bag of marbles gives the experience of one and of many. (Do not use marbles with people who are liable to swallow them.)

> *My heart began to beat and my eyes grew,*
> *though I kept them closed.*

Sound

The ability to keep a beat is a better indicator of later language skills than even a mother's educational background. Rhythm is such an important part of language, and an understanding of rhythm helps us to speak, listen and even read. Our mother's heartbeat is the first beat we encounter, and the beat of a human heart is a very evocative sound to any one of us.

You may be able to find a recording of a heartbeat on the internet to play to illustrate this section of the story, or you may choose to create a beat yourself. Try to choose a deep drum or a large box that will produce a gentle sound rather than a sharp tap. You may be able to alter the sound slightly by adding a muffling element such as a piece of fabric either inside or over the drum. Keep a steady beat to indicate the mother's heartbeat. Allow the story experiencer to join in with creating the beat with you. You can hold their hand to support them in co-creating the beat with you or simply allow them to share the drum with you and beat a rhythm alongside you.

I grew fingers and toes, I swam and I kicked.
My skin was covered with soft lanugo fur.

You can choose to illustrate this section of the story with movement or touch.

Movement

Early on in the womb a baby has a lot of space to swim around and move about. Later in pregnancy their limbs will be curled up to fit inside the relatively small space of the womb, but at nine weeks they are smaller than a little lime and are free to wriggle about in the space. Our proprioceptive sense tells us where our body is in space and our vestibular sense informs us about movement and balance – you can use these senses to illustrate this section of the story by allowing/encouraging/supporting the story experiencer to move around in a space as if they were a foetus moving in the space of a womb.

Touch

Babies in the womb pass through lots of different stages, for example when they first grow they have a tail and webbed toes and fingers! One of these stages is fur. Yes, a baby in the womb will be covered with a soft fur called lanugo fur. This has vanished before a baby is born, but it is fun to think of all the changes a baby has been through before it enters the world. You can illustrate this section of the story with a touch experience of soft downy fur – choose a suitable fur fabric or a long pile velvet to provide the experience.

As my ears developed I began to hear
sounds from outside the womb.

Sound

We can only imagine what noises from outside the womb must sound like to a baby inside the womb. If you have ever put your head underwater at a swimming pool and listened to a conversation going on at the side of the pool you have had the experience of hearing sound made outside of water from within water. It is this sort of distortion of sound that you are looking to create with this stimulus. I have two suggestions as to how you might create the impression of sound being listened to from within water; try them out on yourself or a friend first before sharing them with the story experiencer.

- *Using just your hands:* Place the flats of your hands against the story experiencer's ears and press just hard enough to bend the soft parts of the ear but not so hard that you clamp your hands to the side of their head. As you speak, gently move your hands in small circles or up and down movements. This will create a sibilant sound in competition with your own voice.

- *Using a cardboard cup:* Seal your mouth inside the cardboard cup by pressing it into the soft flesh of your cheek, upper lip and chin. When you speak into the cup your voice will be muted and unclear.

Mummy ate for me. I could taste bitter and sweet.

Taste

A baby's mouth and tongue are one of the first facial features to become operational. A baby in the womb will open its mouth at around ten weeks; inside will be a tiny tongue and the baby can take sips of the amniotic fluid. The baby will taste some of the flavours that the mother is eating; for example, if she eats a lot of spicy foods the baby will become familiar with those flavours. Bitter and sweet tastes are easiest for the baby to distinguish.

You can facilitate bitter and sweet tastes using lemon juice and honey; these can be dripped onto the tongue. If the story experiencer is able to facilitate tastes themselves then offering them a slice of lemon and a sweet such as a marshmallow will be an easy way of providing them with bitter and sweet taste experiences.

The bigger I grew the more squashed I became.
On my birthday Mummy and I worked hard
to bring me into the world.

Touch

During the later stages of pregnancy, the baby does not have as much space to move around inside the womb. It will still stretch and kick but to do so it will have to push against the mother; if you are watching the bump you may see it move as a little foot sticks out and the baby inside has a wriggle. Prior to birth, a baby will be very confined by the womb; its arms and legs will be bent up and curled against its body. You can create this confined feeling for the story experiencer by wrapping them tightly in a piece of fabric – a large scarf or a sheet would be ideal. The story experiencer can push against this wrapping like a baby kicking in the womb or pushing its way out into the world.

And then I was here! Able to stretch out, see,
smell, touch, taste and hear: ready to explore the world.

Multi-sensory!

If you feel that multiple experiences might overwhelm the story experiencer, use the movement of stretching to illustrate this section of the story. If you want to go for the whole caboodle, try providing sight, smell, touch, taste and sound experiences – you could choose ones that are associated with the first moments of life, personal favourites for the story experiencer or a set of strong experiences aimed at invigorating each sense in turn. Here are some suggestions.

- *Sight:* A kaleidoscope, scraps of coloured metallic paper showered in front of the story experiencer's eyes, a rainbow filter on a projection wheel.

- *Smell:* A hot flavoured drink with a sweet aroma such as hot blackcurrant, a zingy scented essential oil on a cotton pad, a spritz of perfume.

- *Touch:* A texture board with a variety of textures attached, a string of knobbly objects, a bucket filled with differently textured items such as a wet sponge at the bottom with shredded paper above it hiding other interesting tactile objects.

- *Taste:* Milk, water, favourite foods or drinks.

- *Sound:* Welcoming words such as 'Hello', the crying of an infant, a big noise like a trumpet fanfare or crash of symbols, entrance music, Happy Birthday song.

FACILITATING THE STIMULI

One egg from Mummy and one sperm from
Daddy and there I was! One cell dividing
and growing inside Mummy's womb.

Pass the single object to the story experiencer and allow them time to experience it.

My heart began to beat and my eyes grew,
though I kept them closed.

Produce the rhythm of a heartbeat using a drum or sonorous cardboard box. If the story experiencer is likely to experience the sound in a passive way, consider where you will be best placed to create the sound – will they be more responsive if they can see your movements? Will they be more responsive if the sound is louder or closer to them? Watch for indications that they are responding to the rhythm – we naturally tap our feet or hands to a beat so try to spot if they begin to produce rhythmic movements.

If the story experiencer is able to co-create the beat or cooperate with creating the beat then allow this to happen. Co-creators can share the drum with you and try to match their beats to yours. If they cooperate, you may be able to help them to create the beat themselves by supporting their arm (or leg – they can make the beat with any part of their body). They may allow you to use their hand to create the beat. Another option can be to create the beat on something on which they can rest their hand (or foot or other body part) – for example, you could use the flat of your palm to create a beat on a lap tray on which they could also rest their hand. They may be able to rest their hand on the drum as you produce the beat. Simply resting the drum in their lap can amplify the experience for them, as they will hear the sound and feel the vibrations of the beat as it is produced.

I grew fingers and toes, I swam and I kicked.
My skin was covered with soft lanugo fur.

Movement
Movement can be anything you like – whatever suits you. You might help the story experiencer to move their limbs; you might be able to move them around using a wheelchair and explore the space in the room where you are sharing the story. For more able story experiencers you could encourage them to make the movements they think a baby might make in the womb.

Touch
Present the fur fabric or velvet against something that will make it easier to feel the pile. Simply handing over a bundle of fabric will not give the sensation of stroking soft fur. Attaching the fabric to a stiff piece of card or wrapping it around a cushion will allow the story experiencer to stroke it and feel its softness. Remember, a touch does not have to be experienced with the hands – feet and faces are also good at touching. If the story experiencer is passive, you can stroke the fabric against their skin to allow them to feel it. A single stroke of the fabric may not be enough for the story experiencer to take on

board the experience; allow time for the sensation to be fully appreciated. Be watchful for the story experiencer's reactions and stop if they appear to dislike the sensation.

As my ears developed I began to hear
sounds from outside the womb.

Choose which method of sound distortion you plan to use with the story experiencer. Think about their preferences when making this decision: will they be distracted or upset by you touching their ears? Is their hearing impaired – will they be able to hear the muted sounds produced by speaking into a cup?

Speak words that you would typically hear around the house or words that someone talking to a bump might use, such as, 'Hello in there, how are you? We cannot wait to meet you.' Decide on what these words will be and make a note of them so that you are able to deliver this sound stimulus in the same way each time you share the story.

Mummy ate for me. I could taste bitter and sweet.

You can offer bitter and sweet taste experiences for the story experiencer to try. Present the foods or liquids in a way that suits your experiencer; for example, in a cup that they will be able to hold or by flavouring mashed potato (which does not fall off spoons easily) with lemon juice or honey. If the story experiencer is unable to eat, you can still present taste experiences by using a pipette to drip a small amount of fluid onto the tongue (just enough so that the tongue is coated). You can create a bitter solution by adding lemon juice to water and a sweet solution by mixing honey and water. Be aware of any allergies the story experiencer may have and choose your experience accordingly.

The bigger I grew the more squashed I became.
On my birthday Mummy and I worked hard
to bring me into the world.

A baby's limbs are all bundled up inside the womb prior to birth; you can facilitate the same sensation for the story experiencer by swaddling them in cloth. A large scarf such as a pashmina, sheet or blanket would do. Do not cover the story experiencer's face or apply pressure anywhere that could hurt them. Be aware of the story experiencer's breathing; your aim is to create a confined feeling not bind them so tightly that it restricts their breathing. If you do not have a blanket or scarf to hand, you might be able to create the same effect using their clothes and just pinching up a little of the fabric in your hand so that the garment is more restrictive.

> *And then I was here! Able to stretch out, see,*
> *smell, touch, taste and hear: ready to explore the world.*

This final section of the story can be facilitated using the movement of stretching or through exploring all of your senses in sequence. To facilitate it supported by movement, you can stretch yourself and indicate for the story experiencer to copy you, or support them physically to extend their limbs in a stretch.

Illustrating this section of the story using multiple stimuli will mean you need to be quite well organized in order to deliver the stimuli smoothly in succession. What you do will depend on the stimuli and the story experiencer. Here is an example:

1. *Sight:* Throw a fist full of coloured paper into the air in front of the story experiencer (then reach for the perfume).

2. *Smell:* Mist the air above the story experiencer with perfume so that it follows the coloured paper as it falls.

3. *Touch:* Lift a texture board so that it sits on the story experiencer's lap to be explored.

4. *Taste:* Remove the texture board and offer the story experiencer their favourite snack.

5. *Sound:* Sing happy birthday as they finish eating their snack.

Having so many stimuli happen one after another can be overwhelming for some story experiencers. You will know if it is too much for them. If you feel that it is then simply illustrating this section with the stretch movement is an easy alternative, or you may opt to pick just a few stimuli or present weakened versions of the various experiences; for example, a multi-coloured sheet of paper, a smell wafted under the nose, a simple touch of their hand, a sip of water and a gentle tune.

The story ends with the person ready to explore the world. If you have an activity planned for after the sensory story this can be a great cue to start it. Suggestions for activities can be found in the next section.

EXPLORATION ACTIVITY
Baby world
When the baby is born it sets about discovering the world using all of its senses; you can choose any sensory experience to form a part of this discovery! However, you might like to think about the sorts of experiences a baby is first likely to encounter – baby clothes, baby lotion, baby powder, baby toys, including those with rattles and flashing lights, baby food and the sound of lullabies or perhaps the vacuum cleaner. The story experiencer can take on the role of the newborn child and experience different scents, tastes, textures, sounds and sights of their new world. You can structure these experiences by presenting a narrative of a baby's day: waking up, hearing their mother, being dressed, eating, playing with toys, being washed, and so on.

CREATIVE ACTIVITIES
Fingers and toes
In the third section of this story the baby's fingers and toes become distinct; until this point in its development a baby's fingers and toes are webbed.

If the story experiencer is physically able to, you can help them explore their fingers and toes by setting them these challenges.

- *Finger challenge:* Balance a penny on the pad of your thumb and pass it to your index finger without using your other hand. If the penny began with heads facing up then it must end up with tails facing up on your index finger. Then pass it from your index finger to your middle finger, again making sure it turns over, so this time it will be heads up. Continue until it rests on your little finger.

- *Toe challenge:* Can you lift up and put down each toe in turn, moving only one toe at a time?

If the story experiencer is not ready for these very difficult challenges yet then you can challenge their fingers and toes with other tasks, such as lifting things up or drawing in lines.

They can use finger painting and toe painting to have fun exploring their fingers and toes. If the story experiencer cannot move their fingers and toes themselves, they can be helped to do so. Here are a few ideas of things to paint with fingers (or toes).

Finger painting ideas

- *Flowers:* Use your fingerprints to create the petals of flowers. Add green stems and leaves to your drawing using a felt-tip pen once the paint has dried. Try using fingerprints to paint grape hyacinths – draw a long stem with a green felt-tip pen, dip your fingers into blue paint and print all the way up the stem on both sides.

- *Trees:* Draw a tree trunk and branches using a brown felt-tip pen. Use your fingerprints, or toe prints to add green leaves to the tree.

- *Christmas decorations:* Use black card or paper as a background for your painting. With a pale-coloured drawing pencil, draw the outlines of a street and houses. Draw zigzag lines between the houses to hang your Christmas lights from. Choose lots of different colours and fingerprint along the lines to be the Christmas lights hanging in the street. You could use the same technique on green card to decorate a Christmas tree with coloured lights.

Healthy eating

When a woman is pregnant it is very important that she eats a healthy diet, as what she is eating will be nourishing both her and the baby. Different foods help our body in different ways. Here is a song you can sing to boost awareness of healthy eating. You can add your own verses to the song. It is very simple – you sing it to the tune of 'Frère Jacques' and the lines repeat so one person can sing them and another copy them. Try eating small amounts of the things mentioned in the song just after each verse.

Healthy eating,
Healthy eating,
Is good for you,
Is good for you,
Drink lots of water,
Drink lots of water,
To keep hydrated,
To keep hydrated.
Healthy eating,

Healthy eating,
Is good for you,
Is good for you,
Eat some oily fish,
Eat some oily fish,
To help your brain,
To help your brain.
Healthy eating,
Healthy eating,
Is good for you,
Is good for you,
Eat lots of vegetables,
Eat lots of vegetables,
To get vitamins,
To get vitamins.
Healthy eating,
Healthy eating,
Is good for you,
Is good for you,
Eat some juicy oranges,
Eat some juicy oranges,
To keep colds away,
To keep colds away.

Make up your own verses. It is easy to do.

DISCOVERY ACTIVITIES
Dividing cells

The story starts with a single cell, which divides. It divides into two cells, which in turn grow and divide into two cells each, making four cells. The four cells become eight, the eight become sixteen, sixteen become thirty-two and so on. This can be hard to picture in our imaginations and very difficult to watch because the cells themselves are very small and hidden away. However, you can create a representation of this using washing-up liquid and a straw. Extra strong bubble mixture will work even better than washing-up liquid. The small straws on the sides of drinks cartons that have diagonally cut ends are also useful when doing this. Here is how to do it.

- Prepare a clean, flat surface that will be easy for everyone to see. The surface needs to be smooth and must be one you do not mind getting washing-up liquid on.

- Dip the end of your straw into the washing-up liquid and blow a single bubble onto the flat surface and say, 'This is the one cell.'

- By keeping your straw inside the bubble you can blow gently to make it grow. Say, 'The cell grows.'

- Remove your straw from the bubble and place it so that its end is in contact with the flat surface on one side of the bubble; draw it smoothly straight through the bubble. This will cut the bubble into two linked bubbles. Say, 'The cell grows and then divides, forming two cells.'

- If you have the small, diagonally cut straw, quickly (as bubbles have a limited shelf life) insert the sharp end of the straw into one of the two bubbles and blow gently a little bit, then repeat with the other bubble. Say, 'The two cells grow.'

- Remove your straw and place it so that its end is in contact with the flat surface, but this time make sure that when you draw it smoothly through the bubbles it will pass through both, cutting them into four. Say, 'The cells grow and divide.'

- As quickly as you can, repeat the process, but this time you will have to draw the straw through the bubbles twice to chop the four bubbles into eight. You can continue doing this for as long as your bubble mixture or washing-up liquid holds out.

- Adding a few drops of food colouring can make the bubbles easier to see. If you have access to an overhead projector, blowing the bubbles on the glass mirror of the projector will allow you to project them onto a wall, making it possible for lots of people to see at once.

Number sequences

It can be fun to explore the sequence of numbers the dividing creates. One way of doing this is by using modelling clay.

Begin by giving the story experiencer a small ball of clay and ask them to divide it in two. Give them a little bit more clay to add to the two pieces of clay they now have and get them to roll the new clay into the existing clay to grow the two balls. You can help them to manipulate the clay. As you are doing this, you can explain the first section of the story in more detail:

'First there was just one cell.' Hand the story experiencer one small ball of clay and give them the time to feel it with their hands.

'That cell divided.' Support the story experiencer in pulling the small ball of clay apart into two pieces.

'Now there are two.' Count the two pieces of clay with the story experiencer.

'Each cell grew.' Add a little clay to each of the two existing pieces. Help the story experiencer to roll the new clay into the old to create two separate balls.

'The two cells...' Count the two balls together '...both divided.' Support the story experiencer in pulling apart the two balls of clay to form four pieces of clay.

Continue in the same way until you run out of clay!

Although this story is well known, people experiencing it for the first time can find it amusing that the cells just keep on dividing. They can share this sense of fun with you as you share the exploration with them.

You can further support your exploration by writing down the numbers you discover or by colouring them in on a hundred square.

You can explore the number sequence in other ways, for example painting dots to represent the cells as they grow and divide. How many times will they be able to divide before there is no longer room on your page? You could use marbles or unit cubes to lay out the sequence, beginning with one, then two cubes, then four and so on, until you run out.

More cognitively able story experiencers may enjoy discussing how these cells come to form the different parts of the body. Looking at pictures of different types of cells can be very interesting: think about nerve cells – they look like little fireworks going off; red blood cells have a dimple in them for carrying oxygen; muscle cells are long and stretchy. You can show the story experiencer the different pictures of cells and ask them to guess which one does which job; this is a good way to get them thinking about the reasons why the cells are different shapes. Could they invent a cell for a particular job? Or draw what they think a particular type of cell might look like? If you are able to get a microscope you can show them the cells in an onion by peeling off a single layer of onion skin and looking at it through the microscope.

Keep the beat

Being able to join in with and keep a beat is an important part of the development of communication. Sharing in creating a beat is a bonding experience, and many cultures use collective drumming as part of traditional rituals.

You can explore further the second section of this story with the story experiencer by sharing beats together. Add interest by creating beats using different things – lots of things you can find around the house will lend themselves to becoming percussion instruments, with a little imagination. It can also be fun to use different parts of the body to keep rhythm: tapping your feet, clapping your hands, slapping your thigh or tapping your cheek while holding your mouth open. Using the body can add a tactile experience to this auditory one, which the story experiencer may enjoy.

You can develop the idea of the heartbeat by listening to your own heartbeat. If you happen to have a stethoscope, that's fantastic, but if not you may find that even a child's plastic toy stethoscope will allow you to hear a heartbeat. Feeling your heartbeat either by placing your hand on your chest or taking your pulse is interesting to people.

Once you have identified your heartbeat, you can try to produce a beat to match it. You can develop this activity by seeing if you can mimic the heartbeats of other animals. Little birds and mice have fantastically fast heartbeats, whereas some larger animals like horses and whales have much slower heartbeats. A blue whale's heart beats only six times a minute. The next activity shows how you can make a game of this exploration.

That is my beat
Preparation

- Print out pictures of different animals from the internet (or use postcards or photographs).

- Look up the heart rates for the different animals and write these on the back of the pictures.

- Try to choose animals with a range of different heartbeats, from the very high to the very low.

Optional extra
Create a heartbeat scale by writing in a continuous line the numbers from zero to the highest heart rate you have for an animal in your set of cards. Divide the line of numbers up into sections and label these according to the speed of the heart rates indicated within the sections, for example, slow, fast, very slow, very fast, etc.

To play the game

- Choose a card and hand it to your partner without looking at the back of the card.

- Your partner looks at the back of the card, so that they know the heartbeats per minute of the animal you have chosen but you do not.

- Create what you think the heartbeat of the animal would sound like using any instrument you want.

- Your partner can tell you whether you are right or wrong or conduct you to increase or decrease your speed.

- If you get the heart rate right, you keep the card with the animal on it. If you fail to get the heart rate right then the card is discarded.

- Swap roles – now your partner chooses a card and gives it to you to look at. They create the beat and you tell them if they have got it right or wrong. At the end of their go, award them the card or discard it.

- Continue to take turns until there are no cards left.

- The winner is the person who has collected the most animal cards.

Alternative version

- Choose two animal cards and read their heart rates. Do not show their heart rates to your partner. Place the cards in front of you and begin to play the beat that matches the heart rate of one of the animals on your cards.

- Your partner must guess which animal's heart rate you are mimicking. If they get it right, they keep the animal card; if they get it wrong, you keep the card. The other card is discarded.

- Take it in turns to be the person guessing until you are out of cards.

You can make this game harder by having more animals for your partner to guess from, for example by choosing three animals at the start. If you choose larger numbers of cards, you may decide to allow your partner more than one guess, for example if you are laying out five cards you might allow your partner two guesses to identify your animal. If you are using large numbers of animals to guess between, instead of discarding the cards that were not chosen, put them back into the main pack (otherwise you will run out of animals too quickly).

✳ To the Centre of the Earth!

This story will place the story experiencer in a capsule and take them on an adventure to the centre of the earth. It has a repeating experience of vibrations through it, which is great for people who enjoy strong touch experiences.

Hold tight! We are starting the drills.
We are going on a journey.
We are going to drill all the way down to the centre of the earth.

Into the wet soil, through the roots of plants and trees, down we go!

We are drilling through rock now, burrowing through the earth's crust.
Water drips through the cracks.
Our drills are working hard.

What is this? Sticky, black and thick, it is oil!
We journey on.

The drills continue through the hard mantle.
The vibrations stop and we are tumbling forward through molten magma.

Our capsule is very hot now;
see the control panel glowing red.

Look! The instruments on our control panel
are spinning wildly: magnetic interference.

Hear the drills beginning to bite again, grinding upon iron and nickel,
we are approaching the earth's core.
We are nearly there!

Suddenly we are weightless, drifting in the scorching centre of the earth.
We are super humans to have survived this journey.
Hurrah!

ABOUT THE STORY

Science fiction has often made the journey to the centre of the earth; Jules Verne's account is the most famous but many other authors have imagined the journey.

This story will work well for someone who uses a wheelchair with a tray attached. If the story experiencer is not a wheelchair user then sitting at a table can help you to create your capsule to adventure in. It is a very tactile story so may also suit someone with a sight or hearing impairment.

RESOURCING THE STORY
Shopping list

- A tray with handles (ideally a metal one)

- A hand whisk or drill with a large chunky bit, for example a square bit

- Wet soil, plant roots, fresh herbs

- Black food colouring, cornflour, water

- Water in a container that it can be slowly poured from

- Large gravel

- Red cellophane and a strong torch

- Cardboard, tinfoil, split pins, a felt-tip pen

Detailed list

Hold tight! We are starting the drills.
We are going on a journey.
We are going to drill all the way down to the centre of the earth.

Touch, proprioception and sound

To create the vibrations in your imaginary capsule as you travel to the centre of the earth you are going to operate a hand drill or whisk between the table, or lap tray, and a tray with handles. If you are worried about scratching your table or lap tray, place a protective cloth over it before setting up for the story.

Ideally, the screen of the capsule will hide the hand whisk from the story experiencer, helping to preserve a little of the mystery of the adventure.

You may want to experiment with different ways of creating the drilling vibrations. If the story experiencer is able to hold on to the handles of the tray then they will prevent it from slipping off the table as you whisk or drill. If they are quite heavy handed then you will need a stronger drilling technique than if they have a lighter touch; for example, using a hand whisk underneath a tray while someone is pressing down hard will be tricky, but turning a hand whisk under a tray lightly balanced above it will be possible.

You are looking to make the tray vibrate and judder as if it is the control panel of a complex drilling machine. Whisks and drills offer a few options. Drill bits come in many different shapes and sizes; a square bit or a particularly lumpy bit will make creating vibrations easy. If you cannot get a hand whisk or a drill then you can try creating the vibrations in other ways, for example putting a ridged surface below the tray and then pulling a large bead or ball on a string over it, which would produce vibrations. Another simple way of creating bumps and vibrations is to get two long lumpy sticks – you can make notches in wood, find sticks from the garden, or even use two wooden spoons. Cross them over one another between the tray and table in an X shape and move each back and forth to create bumps and vibrations. Creating the vibrations using this simpler method will not make the mechanical noise a drill or whisk will make. Depending on who the story experiencer is you may decide this is for the best because they will be able to focus on the story better without background noise, or you may choose to find a way of making a sound representing machinery to add atmosphere to the story – a hairdryer could create a gentle hum and also be useful later on when you want the capsule to get warmer.

Into the wet soil, through the roots of plants and trees, down we go!

Touch, smell and taste

This is your best opportunity within this story to give the story experiencer smell and taste experiences. As your adventurer begins their journey they will be digging down through plants and soil to the rocks below; it is possible that surface plants would get tangled in the drill and be churned into the soil along with the roots and tubas of other plants. Create a tray of foliage or wet earth to explore. If you want the experience to be wholly edible then use mashed vegetables in place of earth. Adding fresh herbs such as lemon balm or mint will provide the story experiencer with smells as well as safe taste options.

If you are not aiming for taste then you can have lots of fun making an earthy exploratory tray with roots, twigs and root vegetables. If you are sharing the story with a dinosaur fan you might be able to add some pretend dinosaur bones or fossils to be discovered.

> *We are drilling through rock now, burrowing through the earth's crust.*
> *Water drips through the cracks.*
> *Our drills are working hard.*

Touch
Choose rocks that will not present a choking hazard if the story experiencer is likely to try and put them into their mouth. Be mindful that rocks can be thrown; if you think this is a possibility then choose smaller rocks or be ready to catch.

> *What is this? Sticky, black and thick, it is oil!*
> *We journey on.*

Touch and taste
There are many ways to create a sticky goo. You can create a texture you think will interest the story experiencer. Remember that oil deposits hidden within the earth's crust may be contaminated with other particles, for example sand and grit, so there is a lot of scope for creating a granular texture to your goo.

One of the simplest ways to create a goo is to use cornflour (in the USA, cornflour is called cornstarch). To create the goo pour cornflour into a bowl, add a few drops of black food colouring and then gradually add water, stirring steadily until you reach a consistency you are happy with. If you want to create something that tastes a little nicer then use condensed milk instead of water – this will give you a thick, sticky, sweet, black goo. For an even simpler, even sweeter method, use black treacle. You will get very sticky!

> *The drills continue through the hard mantle.*
> *The vibrations stop and we are tumbling forward through molten magma.*

Touch, vestibulation and sound
The drill vibrations will be created in the same manner as in the first section of the story. To create the sensation of tumbling you can encourage or support the story experiencer to move in a tumbling manner; this could be rolling over on the floor or moving in loops and circles. If the story experiencer is a wheelchair user then you may be able to steer their wheelchair in loops for them; if they are able to drive their chair, it can still be good for you to

control it for this part of the story, as the adventurers in the capsule would have no control of its tumbling as it falls through the viscous lower mantle and molten outer core.

> *Our capsule is very hot now;*
> *see the control panel glowing red.*

Sight and touch

To make the control panel on your capsule glow red, shine a torch with red cellophane over the front at it. If you are using a hairdryer to create a machinery noise along with your drilling, you can allow the heat from the hairdryer to warm up the tray that is being used as the base of the story experiencer's control panel. As there is no drilling for this part of the story, you could also warm the tray by placing a hot water bottle between the tray and the table – this would also create the rocking sensation of tumbling through dense molten fluid. The centre of the earth reaches temperatures similar to those on the sun; clearly you will not want to expose the story experiencer to dangerously hot things so be careful if you are using boiling water in the hot water bottle or a hairdryer (hold your hand under the flow of air to check the heat, and remember that a temperature that seems bearable can become too hot over time).

> *Look! The instruments on our control panel*
> *are spinning wildly: magnetic interference.*

Sight, touch and proprioception

Making your control panel can be a lot of fun, and it may be something you want to spend some time doing with the story experiencer before setting off on your journey. To create a simple capsule, make a curve or fold of cardboard that can be stood in front of the tray or even attached to it. This can be like the dashboard in a car, with a number of dials on display low down, or you can let your imagination run wild and build a capsule from cardboard boxes big enough to actually climb inside, with windows and buttons. The dials are the important part for this stimulus. The earth's magnetic fields are believed to be caused by currents in the metal of the core of the earth – at this part of your journey you would be within that core and the currents would be all around you, so the magnetic field would not be as stable as it is on the surface of the earth. This magnetic instability would interfere with electronics and so it is likely that the dials in your capsule would spin. To create a spinning dial, mark a circle on the card and notch and number it around the edge so that it could be recording speed or depth. Make a needle out of strong card that will point to the speed or depth. Attach the needle to the centre of the circle using a split pin and turn it a few times to make sure that it will spin easily. You can wrap or glue tin foil around your dial, or over your needle, to make it look like a metallic instrument.

> *Hear the drills beginning to bite again, grinding upon iron and nickel,*
> *we are approaching the earth's core.*
> *We are nearly there!*

Touch and sound
Create the vibrations of the drill in the same manner as before.

> *Suddenly we are weightless, drifting in the scorching centre of the earth.*
> *We are super humans to have survived this journey.*
> *Hurrah!*

Proprioception, vestibulation and sound
Weightlessness would be a very tricky thing to create unless you happen to be sharing the story on the moon or indeed at the centre of the earth. So rather than weightlessness itself we are going to aim for movements similar to those performed by people in zero gravity. If you have ever seen footage of astronauts moving about inside space capsules you will have noticed that their movements are slow and deliberate – they glide and drift. You can be as creative as you like here, but a simple approach would be to have the story experiencer raise their hands (you can support them to do this if they need help). Once their arms and hands are raised they can sway and even spin as if they are drifting and weightless.

Surviving such a journey is impossible, as temperatures at the centre of the earth reach over 5000°C, so to have made it successfully you and the story experiencer really must be super human in some way. These super powers and the success of your journey are worth cheering about, so you can end the story by cheering loudly together.

FACILITATING THE STIMULI

> *Hold tight! We are starting the drills.*

We are going on a journey.
We are going to drill all the way down to the centre of the earth.

Have the story experiencer hold on to the handles of the tray, as if they were safety handles inside their capsule. If they are unable to grasp the handles then simply resting their hands on the tray will work.

Create the vibrations in whichever manner you have chosen.

If you are creating a supporting sound, make sure it is loud enough and located in a place where you and the story experiencer will both be able to hear it. You do not want to have to shout the story because you are being drowned out by the noise of the drill...or maybe you do (but if you do, remember this is a story that is intended to be retold so you might earn yourself a sore throat over time).

Into the wet soil, through the roots of plants and trees, down we go!

Place the tray of soil and plants on top of the tray that is being used as your capsule; allow the story experiencer time to explore its contents and give them time to take in its smells.

We are drilling through rock now, burrowing through the earth's crust.
Water drips through the cracks.
Our drills are working hard.

Exchange the tray of soil and plants for rocks. It may be easier for you to have these on a tray too. You can wet the rocks before giving them to the story experiencer; keeping them in cold water can be good, as the story experiencer will experience the contrast between the warmth of natural fibres and earth and the coolness of stone. Alternatively, you can gently drip water onto the story experiencer's hands as they touch the rocks, as if water were dripping from rocks above them.

What is this? Sticky, black and thick, it is oil!
We journey on.

Trade the rocks for a bowl of gloop and allow time for its exploration. It will probably be handy to have a damp cloth and towel on hand for the end of this experience. Remember that, for the story experiencer, having their hands cleaned and dried is as much a sensory experience as touching sticky goo. Aim to ensure consistency in this experience, just as you would with the others.

> *The drills continue through the hard mantle.*
> *The vibrations stop and we are tumbling forward through molten magma.*

Facilitate the drilling stimuli in the same way as before. You can choose to vary the drilling, for example slow drilling and high-pitched, fast drilling, or to make it consistent throughout the story. It is likely that your choice will be based on the needs of the story experiencer. If you are looking for the story experiencer to be able to anticipate the sensation of drilling then you might want to keep the experience consistent over the story and over different tellings.

> *Our capsule is very hot now;*
> *see the control panel glowing red.*

Be sure that the parts of the control panel that the red light falls on, or lights up, are in a position where they are easy for the story experiencer to feel.

If you have placed a hot water bottle underneath the tray or are directing the flow of air from a hairdryer towards it, allow enough time for the tray to heat up and then enough time for the story experiencer to process the sensation of heat beneath their hands.

> *Look! The instruments on our control panel*
> *are spinning wildly: magnetic interference.*

Make the dial spin by giving it a good push with your fingers; this can be fun to do and you may want to encourage or support the story experiencer to spin the dials for themselves – this will help them to develop their awareness of where their body is in space as they coordinate their senses of sight and proprioception to move their hand towards the needle.

If you want to be really cunning you could attach a paper clip to the end of your needle and use a magnet hidden behind the control panel to cause the needle to move. If you are particularly dedicated to detail, you could have a magnet present during the whole story and gradually move the needle around to show different depths or speeds as you progress towards this part of the story and then move the needle rapidly to indicate the magnetic disturbance. This can be a fun job for a sibling or friend of the story experiencer to be given.

> *Hear the drills beginning to bite again, grinding upon iron and nickel,*
> *we are approaching the earth's core.*
> *We are nearly there!*

Repeat the drill vibration experience, varying it or keeping it consistent as is appropriate to the story experiencer.

> *Suddenly we are weightless, drifting in the scorching centre of the earth.*
> *We are super humans to have survived this journey.*
> *Hurrah!*

If the story experiencer is able to make the weightless movements themselves then make them with them – you are both in the capsule and you are both weightless, so enjoy it!

If the story experiencer needs your support to make the movements then be sure that you know enough about their range of movements to facilitate the movements without hurting them. You can try making smaller movements at first and warming up to larger waving motions.

EXPLORATION ACTIVITIES

There are many sensory experiences to be explored within this story. You can choose to explore one on each telling of the story, select favourites or experience them in sequence. Here are some ideas of things you might like to try.

The earth's surface

Growing on the earth's surface: Before the capsule begins its journey to the centre of the earth, it is perched on the earth's surface – picture it surrounded by flora and fauna. Selecting edible plants and flowers and using these to create a cover of greenery over an object representing the capsule offers your explorer the chance to experience their scents, textures and even flavours as they search for the capsule within. Use a deep bowl or a bucket to hide the capsule so that it cannot immediately be seen.

Mud, mud, glorious mud

Grown-ups might not be so keen on mud unless they are at a beauty salon, but mud can be a fabulous touch experience and with a bit of splatting and delving about it also becomes a sound experience too. You can buy child-friendly compost or clay or simply use mud from the garden. Creating different consistencies of mud will make this experience more interesting for the story experiencer, so try some sloppy, runny mud and some thick, gloopy mud. Dress head to toe in waterproofs if you need to – be a bold adventurer unafraid of getting messy!

Temperature

The capsule gets hotter as it journeys deeper into the earth. You need to be very careful to not use things that are too hot, and be aware that some people are more sensitive to temperature than others, but by using a selection of cool and warm items you will be able to create the experience of different temperatures. Think about using: ice cubes, warm water, hand warmers, a hairdryer and cold metal.

You could also explore the following:

- Things that spin, like the instruments as the capsule reaches the centre of the earth. Find a selection of spinning toys – even spin yourself – and use them to explore what spinning means.

- Make your own super-duper dashboard with lots of different knobs, buttons, switches and dials on it. You can make these using bottle tops and cardboard or find real ones from a junk shop or hardware shop.

CREATIVE ACTIVITY
Layers

The capsule sets out to discover what is underneath the earth's surface. You can create art from discovering what is underneath the surface of a picture. Colour a piece of paper or card with lots of bright colours or use brightly coloured or metallic paper to begin with. Cover your paper with a layer of thick wax crayon, and then use a retractable biro with its nib retracted to draw into it, scratching off the crayon to reveal the colours underneath.

Create your own world using layers of paper mache. Begin with a water balloon (blow it up and tie it but do not put water in it). Tie the balloon on a string and hang it somewhere where it will be low enough for you to work on it. You might need to put newspaper or protective sheeting underneath the balloon to catch any drips.

A simple way to make paper mache is to mix a solution of flour and water and then soak strips of newspaper in it. Wrap the soaked newspaper around the balloon until it is completely covered. Leave it to dry.

You are going to add lots of layers to your balloon, but you need to wait until each is dry before adding the next. Think about ways to make your layers different.

- You could scrunch up dry newspaper and use your paper mache to stick it to the balloon. This would create lumps and hills on your balloon.

- You could colour your paper mache with powder paints or food colouring.

- You could add glitter or sand to your paper mache to create texture.

- You could dip wool or string into your flour and water and wrap these around your balloon.

- Invent your own layers.

When you have added as many layers as you want, wait until they are all completely dry, and then explore what they look like when you open your balloon up. You may be able to use a saw to cut your layered balloon in half; you may be able to dig into its surface as if you are the capsule in the story.

DISCOVERY ACTIVITIES
Research
Make a list of all the different materials the capsule encounters on its journey to the centre of the earth. Use books and the internet to find out what we use all these materials for.

Vibrations
The drill causes the capsule to vibrate, and sound is formed by vibrations in the air. Explore a range of musical instruments and try to identify which part of them vibrates to cause the sound.

Journey
Go on a journey of your own and try to notice the same sorts of things that are noticed in the *To the Centre of the Earth!* story. Think about: what do you see, what sounds do you hear, is any machinery involved in your journey, what temperature is it at the start, middle and end of your journey, do you feel bumps or vibrations?

The Forest of Thorns

Original text by Gwendolen Benjamin, based on the tale of *Sleeping Beauty*.

'It is an old tale, your majesty,' said the attendant, 'from an old time, when fairies still walked the world.'

'At the heart of that forest lies a cursed princess, who pricked her finger on a spindle and was sent to sleep for one hundred years.'

Naturally, the prince's duty was to rescue this damsel but several hours of clambering through the forest of thorns had put a damper on his initial burst of heroics.

Wizened trunks twisted into a heavy canopy that blocked out the sunlight and a century of fallen leaves rotted underfoot.

He knew fairies did not exist anymore, but he was followed by a strange chittering and shadows danced at the edges of his vision.

Sweating in grimy armour, his arms grew heavier each time he swung his sword.

He sat heavily on a root and a burst of sunlight caught his eye amongst the oppressive grey of the forest.

It illuminated a rosebush that had somehow found its way out of the mulch, in full bloom and cheerfully unaware of its surroundings.

The prince hacked his way through another briar patch.

He wasn't sure he could give the sleeping princess happily ever after, but he could start by giving her a rose.

Gwendolen Benjamin has created a new version of this traditional tale especially for this book. In her story, you will find a prince who shows remarkable determination when faced with the challenge of a forest of thorns he must hack through in order to rescue his princess. The prince's persistence in confronting difficulty is a great message to share with people. The fantasy elements of the story lend themselves well to the creation of magical sensory experiences for the story experiencers.

RESOURCING THE STORY
Shopping list

- Glitter

- Paper (silver paper)

- A heavy blanket

- Rose scent (perfume, essential oil, potpourri, a strong smelling flower)

- Salt and a mild herbal tea bag

- A rose (ideally a fresh one, but a fake one would be good for consistency)

- A torch (or daylight in a room that can be dulled, e.g. by drawing curtains)

Optional

- A few metal coat hangers or a musical instrument to create a fairy sound

Detailed list

'It is an old tale, your majesty,' said the attendant, 'from an old time, when fairies still walked the world.'

Sight
Glitter: Choosing an iridescent or pearlized colour of glitter, or mixing several different colours of glitter together, will create a more magical effect than a single bold colour. A low lamp or an LED light source can be used to accentuate the sparkling of the glitter. An alternative to glitter would be to use an indoor sparkler to dance before the story experiencer's eyes.

Touch
Roll a sheet of paper to form a point that is safe to use against someone's skin. Choosing silver paper will make your paper point more needle-like.

Naturally, the prince's duty was to rescue this damsel but several hours of clambering through the forest of thorns had put a damper on his initial burst of heroics.

Movement

This experience is going to be delivered through the story experiencer's body so you need nothing more than for them to be present.

Wizened trunks twisted into a heavy canopy that blocked out the sunlight and a century of fallen leaves rotted underfoot.

Sight/smell

For this experience, you can choose between using a heavy blanket or decomposing leaf matter.

A heavy blanket will be used to form the canopy of leaves overhead. You can of course create the darkness of the blocked-out sunlight in other ways, by turning the lights off in a room where you can achieve blackout for example, but if you are able to use a weighty blanket then you can facilitate the story experiencer's understanding of the word 'heavy.'

Decomposing leaf matter gives off a forest-like scent. If you do not want to use foliage that is actually decomposing, try choosing something that is naturally fragrant, pine needles for example. If you do not have a garden you can borrow from then you will be able to find foresty aromas in places that sell potpourri.

He knew fairies didn't exist anymore, but he was followed by a strange chittering and shadows danced at the edges of his vision.

Sound

You can create a chittering noise with your voice, or choose a musical instrument that you think suits the sound of fairies. If you want to make an instrument yourself, experiment with shaking small beads inside a glass jar or small balls of tin foil in a metal bowl. Jangling a handful of metal coat hangers also makes a magical tinkering sound suitable for fairy chittering. If working with a group, you could explore sounds in a session before beginning to tell the story, and invent a chittering noise all of your own – after all, who knows what fairies sound like?

Sweating in grimy armour, his arms grew heavier each time he swung his sword.

Touch/taste

Add a pinch of salt to warm water and taste to imitate the taste of sweat.

He sat heavily on a root and a burst of sunlight caught his eye amongst the oppressive grey of the forest.

Sight

Use a bright torch to be the shaft of sunlight, or better yet, tell the story in a room which you can make dull by drawing the curtains and let in a real shaft of sunlight at this point (of course, this relies on there being sun outside!).

It illuminated a rosebush that had somehow found its way out of the mulch, in full bloom and cheerfully unaware of its surroundings.

Smell

Finding a rose scent should be easy, as many perfumes have a rose base, and essential oils and potpourri also offer rose scents in abundance. Think about how you are going to store and replenish the scent over multiple tellings of the story. If using potpourri, keep the bag sealed and pour out a little fresh each time you tell the story. If using essential oil, add a couple of drops to a cotton pad and store it in a plastic container, allowing the air inside the container to become fragranced. Many perfumes change their smell over time, and are designed to be smelt on skin, so you may have to use yourself as the smell and spray a little onto your hand. Think about whether you will be wearing the scent through the whole story – this would be appropriate as the prince hacking through the forest might be able to smell the roses in the distance. If you are going to wear the smell through the whole story, consider wearing it on your left hand and keeping that hand back as you facilitate the other stimuli and then presenting it for this section so that there is a marked change in the experience.

The prince hacked his way through another briar patch.

Movement

As with the prince's earlier endeavours, all you need for this experience is the story experiencer.

He wasn't sure he could give the sleeping princess happily ever after, but he could start by giving her a rose.

Sight/scent/touch

Being handed a rose is not necessarily a big sensory experience, a rose is relatively small in our field of vision, unless we get pricked by a thorn (and hopefully you will not be) it is not a big touch experience, and scents vary. You can do your best to make this rose a good sensory experience by choosing one with a bold colour, ensuring it has a strong scent – you could cheat by adding a few drops of essential oil or a spritz of perfume if you think it needs it – and presenting it against a contrasting background. Consider wearing clothes that will make it easy for the story experiencer to see the rose against; for example, if you wear a white t-shirt and hold a red rose in front of you that is going to be a bigger visual experience than if you are wearing a floral top in various pink tones and holding up a rose.

FACILITATING THE STIMULI

'It is an old tale, your majesty,' said the attendant, 'from an old time, when fairies still walked the world.'

Sprinkle glitter across the vision of the story experiencer. If you are sharing the story in a room with dull light, having a low lamp beneath the gaze of the story experiencer can make the glitter twinkle more.

'At the heart of that forest lies a cursed princess, who pricked her finger on a spindle and was sent to sleep for one hundred years.'

Prick the finger of the story experiencer with the paper point. If the story experiencer is able they can mime falling asleep in response to this.

Naturally, the prince's duty was to rescue this damsel but several hours of clambering through the forest of thorns had put a damper on his initial burst of heroics.

Move the story experiencer's legs as if they are clambering. Be aware of their movement range and facilitate this experience in a way that is appropriate to them. If the story experiencer is able to move their own limbs then they can mime clambering through the forest themselves.

Wizened trunks twisted into a heavy canopy that blocked out the sunlight and a century of fallen leaves rotted underfoot.

Hold the heavy blanket over the head of the story experiencer; you can allow it to droop so that some of its weight presses against them. It is entirely appropriate for them to have to lift their hand and push it away so as to be able to see. Or allow the story experiencer time to take in the scent of the decomposing leaf matter.

He knew fairies didn't exist anymore, but he was followed by a strange chittering and shadows danced at the edges of his vision.

The fairies are all around the prince but he does not see them. Create the sound of chittering using your voice, coat hangers, or the instrument of your choosing or creation. Move the sound around to create the impression of the fairies dancing about.

Sweating in grimy armour, his arms grew heavier each time he swung his sword.

Rub some of the salty tea onto the story experiencer's arm. The small particles of herb provide the feeling of the grime against the skin, and the salt will add the taste of sweat should the grime be tasted. Be aware that consuming too much salt is dangerous. One teaspoon in a cup of fluid should not present a problem, but make sure that the story experiencer does not treat the cup as a drink.

He sat heavily on a root and a burst of sunlight caught his eye amongst the oppressive grey of the forest.

Use your torch to create a burst of light, or draw back the curtains in your darkened room.

It illuminated a rosebush that had somehow found its way out of the mulch, in full bloom and cheerfully unaware of its surroundings.

The rosebush is still at a distance from the prince. From where he is he can see it in the light and catch its scent on the breeze. You could allow the rose stimulus from the final line of the story to be visible as you waft the scent of roses under the nose of the story experiencer. Make sure you allow enough time for them to take in the scent. Do not encourage the story experiencer to sniff vigorously as this actually makes the smell weaker. We smell as the scent crosses sensors in our nasal passageways, but sniffing vigorously makes the scent pass by faster so we have less chance of smelling it. Normal breathing, or even slow gentle breathing through the nose, is the best way to pick up a scent.

> *The prince hacked his way through another briar patch.*

Move the story experiencer's limbs as if they are hacking through the briar patch. If the story experiencer is able to move their own limbs then they may mime this action. You can choose whether to match this experience to the previous physical experience, or whether to create a contrasting experience. Matching the experience would mean that on both occasions you assist the story experiencer in moving their legs as if clambering. Creating contrasting experiences would mean that on the first occasion you would support the story experiencer in moving their legs and on this line you would support them in creating a hacking motion with their arms.

> *He wasn't sure he could give the sleeping princess happily ever after, but he could start by giving her a rose.*

Hand the story experiencer the rose. Position yourself so that the story experiencer gets the maximum impact from this exchange (see the description in the detailed stimuli list for further information).

EXPLORATION ACTIVITIES

In *The Forest of Thorns* the prince struggles to get through the forest. All of these exploration activities involve making your way from A to B, and various sensory adventures await.

Fairy footsteps

Create a set of sensory stepping stones by placing items of different textures on the floor. You can place items directly onto the floor or secure them to carpet tiles or cardboard to keep them together. Here are some suggestions:

- sand

- corrugated cardboard with the corrugated bit displayed

- pasta of all different shapes and sizes, cooked and uncooked

- fur fabric

- velvet

- beads in a bag

- cushions

Sprinkle a thin trail of glitter between the stepping stones and have the story experiencer follow in the fairy footsteps. If you have more than one story experiencer, you could place the stepping stones quite far apart and lay different trails using different coloured glitter.

Optional extension: Create some sensory glitter play at the end of the trail of fairy footsteps for the story experiencer to explore. Try sprinkling glitter into a water-play tray with a few drops of food colouring, filling a water bottle with water and glitter to shake like a snow globe or adding glitter to a tray of shaving foam.

For people who are unable to walk, make a fingertip fairy footstep journey by gluing items of different textures on to a large sheet of cardboard and marking a route with glitter.

Clambering journey

This exploration is great for people who are able to propel themselves along the floor but are not able to walk. Collect pillowcases or duvet covers and fill them with different textured items, for example:

- cuddly toys

- pasta

- dried peas

- scented draw liners

- a little talcum powder

- bells

- cord, rope or electrical wire (without the plug on)

- cushions

- balls

- balloons.

Spread the filled pillowcases and duvet covers around on the floor, cover them with different textures of fabric if you have them and allow the story experiencer to have their very own clambering sensory adventure as they move around the room.

Chittering experiences

It is great to include the story experiencer in creating and setting up this experience. Use your imaginations to think of what sort of sound a chittering might be. Set up a route lined with noise-making items. Follow the route and hear the different sounds along it. The items might be:

- plastic bottles filled with different items, dangling on strings
- milk bottle tops, or swatches of tin foil, threaded onto cotton and dangling alongside each other
- bead curtains or chain curtains
- bells
- wind chimes
- metal coat hangers
- empty plastic bottles with their lids on and another empty bottle to hit them with
- sand in a container to roll along
- lentils, split peas, dried peas or pasta in a container to roll or shake
- a coin in a glass jar to roll or shake
- rubber bands of different sizes stretched around a box or margarine tub
- balloon rubber stretched over the top of bottles, tins, pots, and held down with strong rubber bands or duct tape, to tap with the fingertips
- glass beakers filled with different amounts of water to be hit gently with a teaspoon
- beads on a string to be dragged over a selection of metal, plastic and glass containers
- cardboard tube rainmakers – a cardboard tube with straws poked through it and a handful of rice sealed inside it.

CREATIVE ACTIVITIES

Make armour

Create your own armour – this can be as basic or adventurous as you like. For basic armour, use masking tape to secure cardboard boxes or tin foil packets to your body. For more adventurous armour, spend time designing and creating tin-foil-covered cardboard pieces for yourself – consider bib-shaped card structures to form chest armour, tubes to cover the forearms and the shins, shields and even swords.

Once you have your armour on, pretend to be the prince. Go outside and hack through the forest of thorns until your armour is sweaty and grimy.

Make a diorama

In the story, a shaft of sunlight illuminates a rose growing in a clearing in the forest of thorns. You can make a diorama of this scene using a shoebox, some dull coloured card, a green pipe cleaner and a little bit of red or pink tissue paper.

- Cut a variety of tree shapes out of your cardboard. Make sure your trees are not taller than the shoebox, and leave a little bit of extra card on them at the bottom, which can be folded over and used to secure the trees into the shoebox.

- Make two holes in the shoebox: one in the smallest end of the box and one in the lid of the box in the centre, about one third of the way along the lid.

- Use tape or glue to stick your trees in the shoebox, leaving a space where the light from the hole in the lid will fall.

- Use the pipe cleaner and tissue paper to make a rose and attach it in the clearing in your cardboard forest.

- Seal the lid on the box and use the second hole as a viewing hole.

Once you have made the basics of your diorama you could improve it by adding extra little slits into the box to create a little bit of light in other areas of the forest. You could make grass by snipping the edge of paper to fray it, and gluing it in. Try covering the extra holes you create with coloured cellophane (happily, some chocolates come wrapped in cellophane wrappers so it may be necessary to eat sweets while you do this!) – you might be able to create a murky green light in some areas of your diorama and a shaft of golden sunlight above the rose.

DISCOVERY ACTIVITIES
What happened in the beginning?
Gwen's version of the story begins with the princess already slumbering. Find out about how she came to fall asleep by researching the start of the *Sleeping Beauty* story.

What happens next?
There is a little known second part to the story: once the princess wakes up, she and the prince are married and have children but the wicked queen mother tries to have the children cooked so she can eat them for her dinner. Find out what happens by researching this part of the *Sleeping Beauty* story.

What happens in other stories?
Find out about other fairy tales that have trapped princesses in them and spot things that are the same and different between them and this tale. For example, in *The Forest of Thorns*, the princess is trapped in sleep, in *Rapunzel*, the princess is trapped in a tower, and in both stories princes rescue the princesses. Write your own story with some elements that are the same as and some that are different from *The Forest of Thorns*.

To whom would I give a rose?
The prince wants to give the princess a life lived happily ever after, but he knows the best he can do in the moment is to give her a rose. Draw a rose in the middle of a sheet of paper and around it draw the people you would like to make happy. Make a rose and give it to someone you would like to make happy.

PART V

GUEST STORIES

The stories in this section of the book are laid out differently from the stories in the preceding section. Each was written by a guest author with a particular talent for sensory storytelling and they've set out their stories in their own style.

The Haircut

The first story is by Victoria Navin from Rhyming Multisensory Stories, who contributed it despite undergoing treatment for a brain tumour. Her story gives story experiencers the chance to explore in narrative a common aspect of self-care: the haircut, which can be quite daunting for people who process sensory information differently.

The story is intended to give the story experiencer space to explore, the time to get accustomed to things, to understand things within the narrative that might not be present in your average hairdresser's appointment.

The story is told in light-hearted rhyming couplets, using everyday language to create the familiarity and routine of this everyday activity. The exuberance of comparing a chair being raised to flying, and the wearing of a barber's cape to being superman is a joyful nod to the bravery involved in facing sensory challenges.

Victoria suggests the use of a doll as an avatar for story experiencers considering taking part in the sensations involved in this story, but who need to understand the sequence first. This is a great access point for story experiencers able to watch the doll and understand their own experience through this process of witnessing experience.

By telling the story a few times at a relatively steady pace you will be able to orientate story experiencers to what to expect within the narrative. You can then begin to slow the telling down, involving them more actively as participants as they explore the landscape of having a haircut. Victoria's concise advice is rich with ways to allow this exploration to unfurl.

At the end of this story you will find a range of fun suggestions for activities to further explore haircuts – my own favourite is the paper plate haircut!

ABOUT THE STORY

The Haircut is aimed at helping individuals overcome sensory barriers to their haircare.

The story re-creates a salon atmosphere and a haircut experience, and there are lots of opportunities for independent self-care within the sharing of the story. There are also opportunities for choice and exploration within resources – hairstyles, shampoo scents, how to decide when there are so many options...

My hair is growing so long that it's covering my eyes
'I think it's time to get it cut' they say (they're really wise!)

The barber's shop is light and bright and smells a little funny
I feel a nervous feeling, like a tickling in my tummy

The barber is kind and friendly as he sits me on a chair
I feel like I am flying as it pumps up in the air!

The barber offers me a cape, it's good to wear it if I can
I slip it on, and instantly, I feel like superman!

The barber mists water on my hair, to make it slightly damp
Then asks if I just want a trim or a total style revamp!

The barber has to touch my head so he can cut my hair
Shows me the comb and scissors and says we must take care

The barber says words to keep me safe: 'Hands on your lap,' 'Chin up,' 'Keep still'
He tells me that if I want to stop, just tell him and he will

I hear some different noises, scissors snip and clippers buzz
I watch my hair fall to the floor in small tufts of fuzz

It's my choice, but if I like, he will dry my hair

With a big hairdryer that blasts out fast, warm air

The barber sweeps a brush across my neck to remove any loose hair
My haircut over; he says, 'Well done!' then lowers down the chair

I look into the mirror and admire my new haircut
'I'll see you soon' the barber says and out of the shop I strut!

RESOURCING THE STIMULI
Shopping list

- Wig/clip in hair extension/doll

- Hairspray/shampoo/conditioner

- Bolster seat/cushion/air wedge cushion/height-adjustable office chair

- Cape/silky material

- Water/water spray bottle

- Brush/comb/two mirrors, greaseproof/non-stick paper

- Hairdryer

- Shaving brush/makeup brush/paintbrush

FACILITATING THE STORY

My hair is growing so long that it's covering my eyes
'I think it's time to get it cut' they say (they're really wise)

Touch and sight
Present the wig/hair extensions to the story experiencer for them to explore. Would the story experiencer like to wear the wig/hair extensions? Present the mirror so that they can study their 'new' appearance in the reflection.

Alternative activity: Present the doll with their hair loose and untamed, covering the eyes.

The barber's shop is light and bright and smells a little funny
I feel a nervous feeling, like a tickling in my tummy

Smell

Mist a little hairspray onto a cloth/paper towel then waft in the air around the story experiencer.

Alternative activity: Open the lid of the shampoo and waft in the air for the story experiencer to smell the perfumed, fresh scent.

> *The barber is kind and friendly as he sits me on a chair*
> *I feel like I am flying as it pumps up in the air!*

Proprioception and vestibulation

Boost the story experiencer's sitting height by placing a cushion/pillow/bolster seat/air wedge cushion on their chair.

Alternative activity: Sit the story experiencer on an adjustable office chair then gently raise the height.

> *The barber offers me a cape, it's good to wear it if I can*
> *I slip it on, and instantly, I feel like superman!*

Touch, proprioception and self-care skills

Engage the story experiencer's sense of touch as they feel the cool, delicate material of the silky cape.

Model placing the cape around your shoulders. Can the story experiencer place the cape around their shoulders independently? Alternatively, place a towel around the story experiencer's shoulders.

> *The barber mists water on my hair, to make it slightly damp*
> *Then asks if I just want a trim or a total style revamp!*

Touch, proprioception and fine motor skills

Model misting water from the water sprayer onto the story experiencer's hair. Can they copy the action? Mist water onto your hair. Taking the lead of the story experiencer, mist their hair. (Note: If they do not like the sensation of water on their hair or near their face then gently mist onto their hand, arm or foot, if tolerated. Alternatively, hold an umbrella over their head and spray the water onto the umbrella.) Can the story experiencer use their fine motor skills to independently mist water from the water spray bottle onto their own hair?

Provide a mirror to help the story experiencer to guide the mist onto their hair.

The barber has to touch my head so he can cut my hair
Shows me the comb and scissors and says we must take care

Fine motor skills and touch

Model using the comb/brush to style the doll's hair. Offer the comb/brush to the story experiencer to investigate. Can the story experiencer comb/brush the doll's hair independently? Taking the lead of the story experiencer, comb/brush their hair. (Note: If the story experiencer does not like their hair being touched then gently stroke the brush up their arm, back or shoulders. Alternatively, sweep a towel over their hair but do not cover their eyes or face.) Practise self-care skills. Can the story experiencer comb/brush their hair independently?

The barber says words to keep me safe, 'Hands on your lap', 'Chin up', 'Keep still'
He tells me that if I want to stop, just tell him and he will

Sound and sight

Draw the story experiencer's attention to the mirror. Encourage them to practise following your instructions to 'Keep still', 'Hands on your lap', 'Chin up'. Model if necessary.

I hear some different noises, scissors snip and clippers buzz
I watch my hair fall to the floor in small tufts of fuzz

Sound, touch and fine motor skills

Fold a piece of greaseproof paper in half then place over the comb with the 'teeth' pointing away from the fold. Hold the comb at the edges then place the fold of the greaseproof paper to your lips and 'hum' to make a 'buzzing' noise like the clippers. Using a fresh piece of greaseproof paper and a clean comb, can the story experiencer copy your action? If you have two combs, you may wish to explore the sound together. Explore patterns and rhythms.

Alternative activity: Gently massage the story experiencer's head with a battery massager or electric toothbrush.

It's my choice, but if I like, he will dry my hair
With a big hairdryer that blasts out fast, warm air

Touch, sound and fine motor skills

Model drying the doll's hair with the hairdryer. Can the story experiencer copy the action? Starting on a slow speed setting, direct the air from the hairdryer onto your own hair then circulate into the air around the story experiencer. Gradually increase the speed and heat settings. Taking the lead of the story experiencer, direct the air (at a safe distance) towards their hands or feet until they are comfortable with the air blowing on their hair. Explore the heat and speed settings.

> *The barber sweeps a brush across my neck to remove any loose hair*
> *My haircut over; he says, 'Well done!' then lowers down the chair.*

Touch, vestibulation, proprioception

Model sweeping the brush around the back of your head and neck. Present the brush to the story experiencer to investigate independently. Taking the lead of the story experiencer, sweep the brush over their hands, arms or feet, exploring different types of brush strokes (some sensory explorers may seek a firmer touch as the brush may tickle, others may prefer short, gentle strokes).

Build tolerance to having the brush swept around the back of the neck. If earlier in the story you placed a cushion pillow, air wedge cushion or bolster seat on the chair then remove it. If the story experiencer is seated on an adjustable office chair, then lower it. Remove the cape/towel.

> *I look into the mirror and admire my new haircut*
> *'I'll see you soon' the barber says and out of the shop I strut!*

Sight

With the story experiencer looking into one mirror, hold a second mirror behind their head so they can see the back of their hair. Practise fine motor skills. Can the story experiencer manipulate the mirror into the correct position to see the back of their head? (Use hand-over-hand if assistance is required.)

EXPLORATION ACTIVITIES
Sensory exploration bags

Add hair gel/shampoo/conditioner (glitter optional) to a sealable strong, see-through plastic bag (zip wallets work well) and seal securely so that the contents cannot leak.

Present to the story experiencer to investigate and have fun 'squishing' the contents.

Sensory bottles

Half fill a clean, clear plastic bottle with water. Add bobbles, hair clips/accessories/glitter. Seal securely then shake.

Present to the story experiencer to enjoy the cause and effect of the movement of the items inside the bottle when it is moved or shaken.

Sensory bin/tuff tray

Place hair-related items – brush/comb/bobbles/ribbons/bandanas/clip-on hair extensions/scrunchies/rollers /Velcro/bendy-flexi rods/brush – on a tuff tray/container.

Include sensory fabrics and materials that represent hair: wool/shredded paper/stainless steel scourer/fake grass/felt/suede (buzz-cut hair)/ pom pom shakers/pipe cleaners/sheepskin/mohair/camelhair/angora.

Add items to encourage scientific investigation: torch, magnifying glass and mirror.

Layer the tuff tray/container with water and add a little baby shampoo to create bubbles.

Use pasta to represent different types of hair, for example: fusilli pasta for short, curly hair; tagliatelle for long, wavy hair; spaghetti for long, straight hair; vermicelli for fine, wavy hair.

Wigs hats and mirrors

Provide a selection of wigs/hats/clip on hair extensions/Alice bands/bandanas/scrunchies for the story experiencer to wear. Provide a mirror so they can see their reflection and how their appearance changes. Can they show a preference for a specific item?

Hairdryer artwork

Connect a hairdryer or a fan to a switch.

Place a piece of paper inside a cardboard box (to minimize paint splatters) and a squeeze of watered-down paints (or food colouring) onto the paper (use different colours and offer the sensory explorer a choice). Place the pools of colour in a line or randomly.

The story experiencer presses the switch that initiates the hairdryer (held by the facilitator) and the air blows the paint to create a pattern (ensure the hairdryer is at a safe distance from the paint as it is a liquid).

This activity can also be done using a fan.

Barber shop listening game

A quick search on the internet will provide you with access to a library of free audio clips and sound effects. These can be played via your phone, iPad or Kindle, or recorded to be played back on a dictaphone or Talking Tile, Multi Memo Recorder or other device.

Play barber shop/hair salon themed sound effects such as scissors snipping, clippers buzzing, an aerosol canister being sprayed, a hairdryer, people chatting, a telephone ringing, the radio playing in the background, water squirting from a water spray bottle. Can the story experiencer communicate a request for 'more' to listen to a motivating sound again? Can they activate the listening device independently? Can they imitate any of the noises? Record and playback so they can hear their voice. Can they correctly identify the sound either verbally or by selecting the correct prop? Experiment with different levels of sound. Offer the use of headphones.

CREATIVE ACTIVITIES
Paper plate haircuts

This activity will promote creativity, fine motor development and scissor skills.

You will need: paper plates crayons/felts/coloured pencils and scissors.

- Draw a face onto the paper plate.

- Cut the outer 'frilly' edge of the plate three-quarters of the way around until you are left with a piece along the top.

- The story experiencer uses the pencils/crayons/felts to colour the hair then experiment cutting the 'frill' of the plate into different styles.

Grassheads

This activity will connect people to horticulture in a fun way as they watch the hair sprout in a short period of time.

You will need: cress or grass seeds and a pair of tights.

- Cut the foot end off a pair of tights.

- Place the cress/grass seed at the toe end of the tights.

- Fill with soil.

- Secure with a knot.

- Rest on a mug so the end with the seeds is pointing upwards.

- Keep well watered.

- When the grass 'hair' grows, story experiencers can practise cutting it using scissors. Experiment using different containers – clean coconut shells make excellent eco-friendly containers. Empty clean eggshells are ideal as they can sit in an egg cup and a face can be draw onto the egg shell.

Hairstyle pictures

Practise fine motor skills by manipulating play-doh or wool into different hairstyles and fixing them to laminated photos of the sensory explorer or different 'clients'.

Can the story experiencer weave ribbons into the play-doh or wool?

DISCOVERY ACTIVITIES
Role play

Role play is a crucial part of development, providing opportunities to practise imaginative play, communication and language skills, building narrative through acting out scenarios.

Set up a hair salon or barber's shop by placing a chair and desk or small table in front of a mirror. Use cushions as a seat bolster.

Provide a cape or silky material, towels, a water sprayer, brushes, combs, spray-on colours, bobbles, clip-on hair pieces, ribbons, clips and rollers for exploration.

Provide a style head such as a 'Girls World' doll or mop head.

Encourage story experiencers to work together in pairs or groups taking different roles in the salon – for example, the receptionist booking appointments, the hairstylist, the client and the junior making drinks and keeping the salon tidy. This sharing of roles and turn-taking will develop awareness of others' thoughts, feelings and opinions.

Can the story experiencers make badges to identify their different job roles?

Setting up a barber shop role-play area provides an excellent opportunity to work with money, whether it is calculating change or devising a price list for services. Set up an area to sell products such as shampoo and conditioner.

Booking appointments presents opportunities to practise time. Provide a 'learning to tell the time' clock with moveable hands.

Role play also provides an excellent opportunity to facilitate PECS (Picture Exchange Communication System) exchanges.

Sparrow Brings Rain

This next story has been contributed by a hero of mine: Dr Nicola Grove, from Surviving through Story and the OpenStoryTellers Project. When I first began researching my adventures into sensory story land it was Dr Grove's work, together with Keith Park's writing, that inspired and delighted me. I'm thrilled to have contributed a chapter to her book, *Using Storytelling to Support Children and Adults with Special Needs: Transforming Lives Through Telling Tales*, and even more excited that she found time to create a story for this book. When I first found her work I never imagined that one day we would be sharing pages together.

Nicola has a passion for traditional tales, and *Sparrow Brings Rain* is an adaptation of a favourite Zulu tale of hers. It is rich with sensation, repetition and meaning – perfect for a sensory story!

The sun shone bright and hot
Hot hot hot
The plants did not grow
Droop droop droop
They needed rain

The animals came together
They beat the drums
They called the rain goddess up in the sky
Rain goddess
Rain goddess
Bring us rain!
Bring us rain!
But she could not hear them

There was NO rain.
It was hot hot hot

I will go said the big bird, the vulture
He flapped his big big wings

He went high high high
Up up up
Into the sky

But then
It was too far
Down down down came vulture
Oh no!
What shall we do?

I know said the sparrow
I know what to do
I know how to get there

You?

Not on my own, said the sparrow
But with your help
We can get there together
And this is what they did

Sparrow flew onto the back of dove
Dove flew onto the back of vulture

Vulture spread his wings
He flew high high high
When he got tired he flew down down down

Dove spread her wings
She flew high high high
When she got tired she flew down down down

But sparrow kept going
He spread his wings
He flew up up up until he reached the sky

He called the rain goddess

Rain goddess rain goddess
Bring us rain

And rain goddess heard him
And she came
She sent down

The lifegiving rain
To water the ground
And feed the people

Sparrow brought rain
With the help of his friends
What can we do?
With the help of our friends?

ABOUT THE STORY (BY NICOLA GROVE)

I was in South Africa in 2008 to explore representations of disability in tra-ditional stories. This story was told to me personally by Muza Ntanzi, then director of the Credo Mutwa Cultural Village in Soweto, Johannesburg (www. gauteng.net/dinokeng/attractions/credo_mutwa_cultural_village). Credo Mutwa was a well-known writer and cultural historian. Within the village was the Khwakhayalendaba (House of Storytelling). At that point, I had not directly encountered anyone with a disability.

Directly after hearing this story, I visited the Museum of Apartheid (www. apartheidmuseum.org), which was surrounded by craft stalls with all man-ner of enticing attractions. However, I had decided to be very frugal on this trip, and declared to my guide that I was not actually going to buy anything more. We were retracing our steps when my eye was caught by a set of flat woven dishes, reasonably priced. I couldn't resist, and chose one. I got into conversation with the young stall holder, who asked me about the small charm hanging around my neck. The silver charm was the logo of the Key Centre for children with autism (www.thekeyschool.org), a kind gift after I had given a talk to the teachers. 'What is autism?' he asked. I explained as best I could. 'I understand something of this,' he said, 'because I have a sister who is mongoloid. She is 12. She just sits at home all day. I think she should go to art school because she loves to draw. But my mother is not sure. What should I do?'

I felt completely inadequate. It came into my mind to share the story I had just heard, and said at the end that maybe he was the vulture. He immediately responded, 'My mother is the dove and my sister is the sparrow. With the right support, she can achieve what she wants.' I took their details to pass on to some of the relevant organizations, and gave him some money to buy her a gift from me. 'What can I get her?' he asked. 'Beads – a necklace?' 'No, she is not interested, she just throws them away.' 'How about drawing materials – or some music?' His face lit up, 'Music, of course. She loves classical music – her favourite is Tchaikovsky!'

I subsequently told the story in Pretoria, first to a group of adults ranging in age from the early twenties to their seventies, who had survived strokes and brain injury, and then in a special school.

The adults apparently had an animated discussion about the story the week after my visit. One man said, 'I can relate to all the birds in the story. I used to feel like the vulture and now I feel like the sparrow.' Another man said that he felt like both sometimes. The discussion revolved around roles of people with disabilities and their supporters, and the story was felt to have had a profound effect.

In school, I asked children who had faced life challenges with support, to stand up and share their stories. Petey (not his real name) had just arrived and was dealing with a new environment well. At the end, he hugged his friend and shouted 'I'm going to teach you to fly!'

MESSAGES

Stories told in African cultures are designed to convey a message about how we should live our lives. These can of course vary (for Muza Ntanzi, the story showed how Zulu culture prefigured the space race, because there were three original rockets to the moon). The message of collective action is one that is frequently encountered in these folktales and is especially relevant to story experiencers and their network of support. It implicitly reinforces the social model of disability (www.learningdisabilities.org.uk/learning-disa-bilities/a-to-z/s/social-model-disability). We can overcome barriers, and we should never underestimate what a person can achieve.

RESOURCING THE STIMULI
Shopping list

- Drum (preferably an African style)

- LED lamp or torch

- Rain maker instrument

- Large cut-out pictures of a vulture, dove and sparrow, mounted on sticks

- Water spray or in bottle (drops are shaken, not sprayed)

- Large fan or fabric that can be flapped to represent wings

- Small bundle of feathers to represent the sparrow

- Small bird-cheeping sound maker (or go mad and buy one of the delightful RSPB singing birds from https://shopping.rspb.org.uk/singing-soft-toys)

Optional

- Heated pad to simulate the warmth of the sun – long strip of cloth or ropes that participants can hold to represent grouping up as the three birds

- CD or internet access for traditional Zulu songs (www.mamalisa.com/?t=el&lang=Zulu)

- Plants for the introduction – maybe ones that story experiencers have planted and watered themselves

- BIGmack communication aid can help with call and response

The sensory stimuli and how to use them
Sound

- Use the drum to introduce and close the session.

- Make the sound of the bird tweeting, or of the soft toy sparrow for the voice of the sparrow.

- Use the rain maker for the sound of the rain when it comes.

Note that for *severely hearing impaired/deaf participants* sound is experienced as vibration and rhythm. High frequency sounds like the cheeping are unlikely to be perceptible. You need additional cues such as skin sensation, movement or signing. The cheeping could be represented by rhythmic tapping of a forefinger on their hand, paired with the soft toy or feathers.

Sight

- Show the bird cut-outs, name them and fly them around the group.

- For a light source for the sun, ideally use LED lamps, or a torch would work. You can choose to make your light source more sun-like by cutting out a disc of yellow tracing paper or tissue paper and attaching this to the front of the light source.

Touch/skin sensations

- For a feeling of warmth, use the light shining on the hand, or the heat pad.

- Gently shake water drops from above on hands (ensure tactile defensive individuals are comfortable with this). Put on plant leaves and feel the difference between dry and wet.

- Pass round feathers to touch or hold in cupped hands like a small bird, or if you have the soft toy, pass it round to be activated, stroked and enjoyed.

- Use a fan or cloth to represent beating wings and air on skin.

Proprioception and movement

- Show the impact of sun and rain on the plants, and the movement of the birds by drooping arms down and rising arms high (supported if need be)/standing and crouching.

- Move arms to simulate wings.

Perkins School for the Blind at www.perkinselearning.org gives great advice for those who are deaf/blind.

Tactile modelling

Support the individual to feel you moving, as a model (participants can also pair up and support each other).

Co-active movement

Support the person to move with you, so that their moving limb/body is directly in touch with your moving limb/body. Always negotiate this with the individual. Never push or grab. Control must stay with the person – this is *not* moving their limbs as though they were puppets! You support from beneath, with a very gentle movement.

Using key signs can help support people to understand the main components of this story. You can look up words such as SUN, RAIN, BIRD, BIG, SMALL,

UP, DOWN, SKY, GROW, CALL, HELP, FRIEND online in the British Sign Language Dictionary at www.signbsl.com) or use key word sign resources such as Signalong (https://signalong.org.uk) or Makaton (https://makaton.org).

FACILITATING THE STIMULI

Prior to beginning the story:

Practise some of the movements and signs if you are using them, and the sounds in the story (e.g. The rainmaker hand game).

Pass around the birds so that everyone is familiar with them before you start to tell the story.

You will also need to spend some time setting up the foundation so that everyone understands why the birds have to fly to heaven. Here is a suggested format.

> *For plants to grow to give us food*
>
> *We need sun and we need rain*
>
> *Here is the sun [shine the light/torch, allow participants to feel the warmth]*
>
> *Here is the rain [shake waterdrops on hands]*
>
> *Here are the plants [pass around plants: you could have one that has withered and gone brown to feel the difference]*
>
> *With enough sun and enough rain the plants grow tall [move hands up, stand and reach up]. Yes! Great, hooray!*
>
> *Too much sun and the plants wither [droop downwards]. Oh dear, oh no*

Note: In the section that follows, there is a shorter and simpler version omitting the flights of the vulture and dove, changing tense and voice. This provides a good starting point to expand the story later on.

INTRODUCING THE STORY

Explain that this is a Zulu story from Africa, and this is the sound of the Zulu drums (drumbeats).

The call and response chant is of course traditional in African storytelling. The 'Yes we're ready' response can be recorded on a BIGmack.

Play with the pitch, pace and volume of your voice for the three antici-patory calls.

Are you ready?
YES we're ready

Are you ready?
YES we're ready

Are you ready?
YES we're ready

Then
We'll
Tell
This
Story
Now.

The table below gives at-a-glance information about which prop to use with which section of the story and what to do with it.

SENTENCE	PROP/ACTION	SENSE	NOTES
The sun shone bright and hot *hot hot hot*	Torch/light/heat pad	Sight/touch	Leave enough time to establish the sense of heat... phew...too hot...
The plants did not grow droop droop droop	Flop bodies downward	Proprioception/ movement	Flop is another nice word here!
Rain goddess, rain goddess, bring us rain	Drum	Sound	Repeat this several times, alternating sound and silence
But she could hear them	Silence	Sound	
There was NO rain. *It was hot hot hot*	Torch/light/heat pad	Sight Skin sensation	
Who will fly/up to the sky/to tell the goddess/to bring the rain		Hearing, rhythm	Can be done as call and response on a BIGmack

SENTENCE	PROP/ACTION	SENSE	NOTES
I will go said the big bird, the vulture	Cheeping sound – sparrow	Hearing/touch	For deaf children, let them hold and stroke the feathers/bird
Not on my own, said the sparrow *But with your help*			Said by staff. Wait for reactions – you can draw this out and dramatize
We can get there together	Show the dove picture	Sight	For deaf children, have two fans, one large for vulture and one small. Use hand under hand signing to show small wings – hands outstretched in front of you
We can get there together	Show the vulture picture	Hearing/touch	Big wings – arms extended from elbow, beating more vigorously
Sparrow flew onto the back of dove	Co-active movement	Proprioception/movement	Line up in threes, one behind the other, or reach out hands to touch, or use a large cloth to link together
Dove flew onto the back of vulture		Proprioception/movement	
He flew high high high	Co-active movement: reach up; use large fan or fabric flapping to represent movement of bird	Proprioception/movement	
When he got tired he flew down down down *When she got tired she flew down down down*	Co-active movement: reach up; use large fan to represent movement of bird	Proprioception/movement	
But sparrow kept going	Use the small feather and move it as if flying up by cheek of child	Touch	
He called the rain goddess	Bird cheeping	Sound	

Rain goddess, rain goddess *Bring us rain*	Drum	Hearing	
And rain goddess heard him *She sent down* *The lifegiving rain*	Shake water drops Make rain sound with rain maker	Touch/sound	Sound and sensation go together for rain; one without the other means water or rattle…
To water the ground		Sound	
And feed the people	Stand up/raise arms high	Proprioception/ movement	
Sparrow brought rain *With the help of his friends* *What can we do* *With the help of our friends*	Closing rhythmic poem	Sound	This is where you can share stories of how you all support each other

EXPLORATION ACTIVITIES
Birds

- Collect different feathers to touch, feel and wave. Make sure these are not *too* small, and wash them in gentle detergent first.

- Set up a bird table or bird feeder and keep a record of the visits.

- Make bird kites (many instructions for simple ways to do this online).

Rain

- Take a tray and fill it with sand (you can warm it in the sun or in a gentle oven). Feel the sand, play with it, and name the sensations – warm, dry, tickly.

- Use a water spray with cool (not cold) water and spray hands with it, again naming the sensations – *cool, wet, drops.*

- Now spray the sand and play with it again! *Squidgy, sticky, clay…*

- When it rains, take everyone outside to experience the sensations.

Go for a walk in the rain, touch and smell plants and leaves that are wet from rain.

Rainmaker game

Model this for participants to copy. Starting quietly, increase the noise level to simulate a rainstorm turning into thunder and lightning, and then fading away:

1. Rub your two hands together, making a very soft sound.

2. Tap two fingers together.

3. Clap hands softly.

4. Slap knees.

5. Stamp feet.

6. Slap knees or clap and stamp feet at the same time as loudly as you can.

7. Work back through steps 5–1, decreasing the sound level as you go.

CREATIVE ACTIVITIES
Book making

Collect the stories of how you help each other in a book (could be made into a sensory book) with the sparrow, dove and vulture on the cover. See www. storysharing.org.uk for how to enable people to share experiences through co-telling.

Artwork

- Create a collage to illustrate the story, using lots of tactile materials.

- Create a photo montage of everyone feeling hot in the sun, cool in the rain, drinking juices or drinks you have made together; and of your plants withering and growing!

Drama

- Create a performance by dramatizing *Sparrow Brings Rain*, along with some of the personal stories.

- Add in music with drums, compose a song.

DISCOVERY ACTIVITIES

This is a perfect opportunity to find out more about African countries and Zulu culture. The Zulu tribe is based in South Africa. You may be able to find local storytellers, musicians, dancers and artists who can visit to share their knowledge and skills: https://africanactivities.org.uk/storytelling-workshops-for-schools.

Song

This lovely Zulu rain chant is available at www.funikijam.com, and at www.mamalisa.com/?t=es&p=4875.

Imvula, imvula:
Chapha chapha, chapha
Imvula, imvula,
Chapha, chapha, chapha
Imanz' impahla yam.
Imanz' impahla yam.
Gqum, Gqum,
Liya-dudu-ma
Gqum, Gqum,
Liya-dudu-ma
Imanz' impahla yam
Imanz' impahla yam
It's raining, it's raining
Chapha chapha chapha
It's raining, it's raining,
Chapha chapha chapha
My clothes are getting wet.
My clothes are getting wet.
Ka-boum, Ka-boum
It's thundering!
Ka-boum, Ka-boum
It's thundering!
My clothes are getting wet.
My clothes are getting wet

Traditional games: Mbube Mbube ('Mboo-bay Mboo-bay')

Help the lion (*mbube*) to find and catch a deer (*impala*). Stand in a circle. Two people are in the middle, both blindfolded: one is the lion and one is the impala. Spin the players around. The watchers call out to the lion, 'mbube, mbube!' getting quicker and louder as the impala gets closer to the lion, and softer and slower as the impala moves away. If the lion fails to catch the impala, a new lion is chosen, and if the lion catches the impala, a new impala is chosen.

As many individuals won't like blindfolds, it is possible to play with only a staff member/supporter blindfolded in the role of the lion.

Find out more about this and other games you could play at https://our-pastimes.com/traditional-african-childrens-games-13583164.html and https://africa.com/best-african-games.

Beadwork
Small beads are a problem, so use large ones in traditional Zulu colours (green, red, yellow, blue, black, white) to create necklaces. Paint some pictures to represent the zigzag patterns of beadwork. For inspiration visit https://zulubeading.weebly.com/method.html.

Food
Maize, pumpkin and sweet potato are traditional foods: https://eshowe.com/zulu-food.

To find out more about traditional Zulua dance visit: https://dancefans.cultu.be/zulu-dance.

To understand more about the long (and frankly shameful) relationship between Britain and South Africa and the Zulu peoples, read David Olusoga's book, *Black and British: A Forgotten History* (2017).

Dr Plankenstein's Super Serum
This story is written by Pete Wells, a man who embodies the joy inherent in sensory stories. His tales are always rambunctious, always silly, sometimes rude, and, at their heart, fun – fun for all people, of all ages and all abilities. Nothing gets between Pete and having a great time, celebrating being who you are and being alive. I know you will hear Pete's enthusiasm through his words. This story is a call for everyone to come forwards, to show what they've got, to let loose and have fun and be celebrated for being who they are how they are. Pete is a superhero of sensory stories. You can listen to him on his podcast *The Special Storyteller* where he shares sensory stories and explodes them into a cascade of ideas that can be used for further engagement and enjoyment with the stories.

You can find Pete's Facebook page The Special Storyteller at https://
bit.ly/366UfZO, and his podcast and loads more sensory stories at https://
sensorystoriespodcast.com.

Doctor Plankenstein's Super Serum, has been left out in the lab!
It takes ordinary people, and makes them SUPER fab!

It makes superheroes SUPER! It makes supervillains BAD!
So let's just have a little taste… I'm sure he won't be mad!

It fizzles and it crackles, as this potion hits your tongue!
Now your superhero journey, has only just begun…

Has it given you super strength? Is that your superpower?
Can you use your muscles, to knock down this mighty tower?

Or has it given you X-Ray eyes? My gosh, oh dearie me!
Look into this mirror, and tell me what you see!

Has it given you super speed? Perhaps now you can zoom?
Let's see how fast you can go, around and round this room!

Has it given you mega smell? Smelling things from far away?
Which one smells the nicest? Which smell is best you'd say?

Or perhaps now you're invisible? Are you now hard to see?
Where has our hero gone? Where can our hero be!?!

Or is it super hearing? Is that the power you've found?
Can you use your super ears, to find a tiny sound?

Doctor Plankenstein enters his lab, picks up his super flask!
What superpowers does it give? The time has come to ask!

He says…

'It's my bottle of pop from my packed lunch! Its superpower rating is zero!
But look at all those things you've done! You're ALREADY a superhero!'

ABOUT THE STORY (BY PETE WELLS)

This sensory story is set in the world of superheroes! Some practitioners
believe that sensory stories should be grounded firmly in reality, as abstract
or fictional ideas can be beyond the comprehension of some of the people we

work with as storytellers. However, it is my understanding that superheroes are remarkable people; they are people with special gifts and the power to delight and amaze! They show courage, great strength and often overcome immeasurable odds. I would argue that in our profession many of the children and adults I have the honour to work with have achieved all of these things and more! So, it is with great pride, confidence and absolutely no apology that I present this rather silly story!

This tale has been written so that it can be highly personalized. Several of the sensory props are very adaptable, so you can use whatever stimulus motivates the particular superhero you are working with.

The story is also non-linear, which means it can be told in a variety of ways and with a limited set of props. Barring the initial and final verses, you can tell this story in whatever order you like, meaning you can carousel the props to reduce wait times for the people exploring the story with you. You may also wish to set your props up in different stations around your story-sharing environment, perhaps with a different coloured or tasting super serum at each station, allowing your superheroes to enjoy a number of tastes before undertaking a particular task. Also, of course, it means you can remove any potentially unsuitable tasks, or shorten the story if required.

A final note, this story was very much written with the self-esteem and wellbeing (both mental and physical) of your young, or not-so-young, super-heroes in mind. Be sure to celebrate all the successes it will bring!

RESOURCING THE STIMULI
Shopping list

- Fizzy drink or popping candy/sherbet

- Blocks

- Mirror or iPad with Snapchat or Instagram

- Vortex cubes or tubs with fruit

- Blanket/voile

- Percussion instrument or single switch communicator

- Flask

FACILITATING THE STORY
Before you start
Be sure to have a storytelling routine. Is there a particular location where you do it? A piece of music, individualized object of reference or position that lets the superhero know that it's story time? You can try using specific sounds and lighting to create an ambiance or have a key phrase or action. Knowing that it's story time is vital...

> *Doctor Plankenstein's Super Serum, has been left out in the lab!*
> *It takes ordinary people, and makes them SUPER fab!*
>
> *It makes superheroes SUPER! It makes supervillains BAD!*
> *So let's just have a little taste... I'm sure he won't be mad!*

Visual, smell, sound
Present the bottle of Super Serum to your superhero. If it is a fizzy drink, you may open it (or invite your hero to open it if they can) so they hear a hiss and get a smell of the delightful potion to come.

Tasting the Super Serum!

> *It fizzles and it crackles, as this potion hits your tongue!*
> *Now your superhero journey, has only just begun...*

Taste
Start off by wetting your budding superhero's whistle with a stimulating, highly motivational taste! Dr Plankenstein's secret serum could be your hero's favourite fizzy drink, though obviously your choice of beverage does not have to be carbonated if this could cause digestion issues. Try to give the hero a choice between different sodas or drinks to facilitate that vital intentional communication and to help with independence skills later on in life. If your superhero is using an augmentative communication strategy, then obviously it is extremely beneficial to get them to ask for the drink or potion they require!

Of course, some of our superheroes will be nil-by-mouth, so feel free to put thickened juice or puree into a weaning pouch and allow your hero to taste that. Alternatively, the usual suspects of lip balms or very viscous and tasty liquids (e.g. syrup or honey) being rubbed on the lip will also do the job here.

Taste, sound, touch

The story states that Professor Plankenstein's Super Serum fizzles and crackles, and what better way to explore this than through delicious popping candy? If your superhero can tolerate popping candy then this can be a literal sensory explosion in their mouth! The pleasant taste, coupled with the amplified aural excitement of the popping, as well the as the tactile sensation of the effervescence, can be highly stimulating and motivational. Please note, you may wish to use sherbet here, which will have a similar effect.

Visual, smell

There are many very exciting ways to make your own visually stimulating sensory potions or calming jars. For this particular story, a conical flask or simple plastic bottle filled with glitter, water beads, coloured gels and other items can be extremely visually stimulating. You should encourage your superhero to engage their hand-eye coordination and motor skills to swill and tumble the liquid in the flask. To add an extra sensory dimension, add a smell and invite your potential superhero to identify what it is – removing the lids from jars or tops from bottles being an extremely handy skill. Is it strawberry? Mint? Orange? You will find all of these smells readily available in the home baking aisle of your local supermarket.

Super strength

> *Has it given you super strength? Is that your superpower?*
> *Can you use your muscles, to knock down this mighty tower?*

Your superhero in training may have acquired super strength from Dr Plankenstein's potion. Let's put this to the test...

Proprioception, sound

Your superhero may possess the strength of the Hulk, so try SMASHING some items! Try setting up a tower of blocks, or if your superhero is able, get *them* to build a tower, which they can then knock down with their super strength! This is irresistible and great for exploring anticipation and cause and effect.

Of course, as with all activities, your reaction is key here. So where appropriate, you should make a huge fuss (positive or negative!) of your superhero when they knock down the tower. You can also promote some pre-verbal communication here with a hearty roar as they smush the tower!

Proprioception, tactile

There are many different ways of testing the new-found super strength of your superhero. These include:

Stretchy fabrics: Practitioners who teach dance massage or facilitate physiotherapy programs may have come across all manner of stretchy fabrics which are great for manipulation or a little game of tug-of-war. This can really get those limbs going and stretch those muscles out. If you don't have specialist fabrics, try using a stretchy, rubber 'colourful caterpillar' – these are readily available online.

Cuddle loops: These are fairly inexpensive, stretchable lycra cocoons that offer a snug swaddling effect which many of our heroes will enjoy. Your superhero can wear one of these then push and manipulate it to show off their super strength!

Lifting, pushing or pulling: Lifting and carrying items can be great for encouraging pincer and tripod grips as well as other important holds. Your heroes may enjoy the resistance they feel with weighted items. Similarly, pushing, pulling or any manipulation of specialist boards, equipment or even people could be a way for your superheroes to show their strength (as well as practising proprioceptive skills).

As ever, this sensory prompt really displays the versatility and a high degree of personalization that sensory stories can offer.

X-ray vision

> *Or has it given you X-Ray eyes? My gosh, oh dearie me!*
> *Look into this mirror, and tell me what you see!*

The rationale of this line is to experiment with your superhero's vision! There are numerous ways to quickly and easily manipulate your hero's vision; here are a few:

Visual

Coloured transparencies: Using different coloured transparencies can instantly change the room for your superhero and be a strong visual stimulus. There are numerous studies that show that seeing life through different colours can have a significant effect on emotions and even understanding. So, try exploring the world through different coloured lenses and see how this makes your hero feel...

Visual, proprioception, vestibular

Selfie mask apps: Applications such as Snapchat or Instagram have some amazing in-built facial manipulation masks that many of our superheroes find absolutely mesmerizing! As part of early development, neurotypical humans are instinctively drawn to the human face. Similarly, many of our heroes will interact for prolonged periods of time with their 'reflection' in a facial app. The joy of these apps is that they contain in-built, often interactive masks that can transform your hero into anything! For this particular story, you can use various x-ray masks that will turn your superhero into an impressive-looking x-ray style image or even a realistic-looking skeleton! Many of these masks or lenses will interact with your superhero too, opening its mouth, blinking or swaying when they do. This is a great way to empower your superhero to facilitate some meaningful interaction, and can be helpful for giving them the prerequisite skills for activities such as intensive interaction and pre-verbal communication.

Visual, tactile, proprioception

Non-technical x-ray vision: Of course, you don't have to go all high tech. A mirror with a paper skull stuck on it, or some skeletal Halloween gloves will do the job of giving your hero that awesome x-ray vision! Alternatively, you could use a mirror with a magnifying glass to distort your hero's vision of themselves...

Super speed!

Has it given you super speed? Perhaps now you can zoom?
Let's see how fast you can go, around and round this room!

Vestibular

Vestibular motion is very important in sensory stories and it's often one of the forgotten stimuli! Many of our superheroes will welcome a movement break during the story and may well need to burn off some energy before re-engaging with some focused work. This part of the story is designed to let your superheroes explore their learning environment and will obviously be adapted to the physical needs of your particular heroes. If you have ambulant heroes then a couple of laps around your learning environment could be great fun. You can add a numeracy element to this by introducing a timer or stopwatch or inviting your crusaders to count how quickly they can safely traverse the learning environment. Please note, this doesn't have to be competitive or speedy, a hero parade around the learning space can be great fun and a wonderful opportunity for real interaction with peers.

Non-ambulant learners may enjoy being pushed around the learning environment. This may be very quickly or somewhat more slowly, with a number of stations of engaging sensory items or activities to explore as they 'walk' around the room. This part of the activity could be particularly useful for learners who use walking frames, floor surfers, walkers or powered wheelchairs.

All senses

Your superhero may possess super-speed in any other activity. This could be something developmental such as threading, posting blocks into an activity board, completing an inset board or just something highly motivational like clapping, ripping paper, eating jelly, whatever your hero enjoys. Again, this is a part of the story that can be highly personalized!

Super smell!

> *Has it given you mega smell? Smelling things from far away?*
> *Which one smells the nicest? Which smell is best you'd say?*

Here we are going to see if your superhero has developed the power of super smelling! Quite what the benefits of this superpower would be, I do not know, but who am I to question the wisdom of the esteemed Dr Plankenstein?

Smell

Smell is super important as it is linked to the limbic system, a very powerful part of the brain linked to, among other things, memory and our flight or fight response. This makes smell very powerful for promoting pre- and post-verbal communication as well as triggering memories and emotions.

My go-to for smells are vortex cubes by a company called AromaPrime. These little boxes pack a very powerful aroma, of which there are a choice of hundreds. If treated with respect, these little boxes can last for years and can really invoke a powerful reaction from your superheroes.

For this part of the activity, try to have a selection of smells for your hero to detect, and if possible identify. This can be using the aforementioned vortex cubes or by putting real items, for example strong smelling fruits such as strawberry or pineapple, into small tubs and allowing the hero to have a whiff. If your superhero is able, you may ask them to discriminate between smells, identifying verbally, from a symbol or real object, what the item is they are currently smelling.

Proprioception
Alternatively, the focus may be on the problem-solving skills – can your hero remove the lid from a jar or tub and smell the contents inside?

Invisibility!

> *Or perhaps now you're invisible? Are you now hard to see?*
> *Where has our hero gone? Where can our hero be!?!*

Lots of fun to be had here as you explore important concepts such as peeka-boo, hide and seek, object permanence and your hero's level of egocentricity.

Visual, proprioception
In this part of the story, you may wish to cover your hero with a blanket or voile before exclaiming in your best Oscar-winning voice 'Where has our hero gone? Where can our hero be!?!' The instant visual change from being able to see the room to being covered will be stark, and will be very stimulating for some superheroes! If your hero is a little timid, then you can use voile which is semi-transparent so they should be able to see their trusted adults in the room (but of course, the trusted adults can't see them!).

During this activity, you will probably engage in some form of peekaboo activity, which has been a staple and instinctive game in child development since child development began! This kind of game serves as a good problem-solving activity as the hero invariably removes their covering, which incorporates some gross-motor movement and coordination.

Alternatively, you can go the whole hog and have a quick game of hide and seek. This obviously incorporates a range of skills and cognitive processes and is great fun to boot!

Super hearing!

> *Or is it super hearing? Is that the power you've found?*
> *Can you use your super ears, to find a tiny sound?*

Another very open-ended activity awaits here, where the storyteller should choose a sound that they know appeals to the superhero. This can be bells, a whoopee cushion, percussion instruments, a tuning fork, a favourite song recorded on a sound switch, a squeaky toy or duck quack...whatever wonderful sound motivates your particular hero! The benefit to using a high-tech communication aid, such as a BIGmack, or percussion instruments or a tuning fork, is that the sound can be stretched out, allowing your superhero the processing time they may need to tune into it and hopefully locate it.

Try making your sound in different areas around your superhero – initially, in the line of vision, then either side of the head and out of their field of view. Make sure that you are confident there will be no seizure activity when exploring sound with your superhero!

The Doctor!

Doctor Plankenstein enters his lab, picks up his super flask!
What superpowers does it give? The time has come to ask!

Visual, taste, smell, proprioception

Here your superhero can manipulate Dr Plankenstein's flask. This can be a sensory bottle as described in the second line of the activity or a real flask where they can try unscrewing a lid. Ensure that your flask contains something nice to smell and/or taste to reward your caped crusader for their magnificent independence skills!

Sound, tactile, proprioception

The time has come to ask what powers the peculiar potion possesses! This should be achieved in a way that most benefits your superhero. This could be any of the following:

- sign
- putting together a visual sentence or symbol strip
- using a single (or more) switch communicator such as a BIGmack or Go Talk
- eye pointing
- high or low-tech communication aids
- verbalization.

The twist!

> *'It's my bottle of pop from my packed lunch! Its superpower rating is zero! Look at all those things you've done! You're already a superhero!'*

I always prefer to end my stories with an extended activity designed to give time for reflection and recap if necessary. Here are some ideas…

Sound, touch, proprioception

We should celebrate the fact that your protagonist is a *real* superhero with a big cheer, euphoric music, much high-fiving, waving, clapping of hands and hugs all round! These interactions may well promote a sense of togetherness, achievement and wellbeing. Please note – some may not enjoy this, so it is important to know your heroes well!

Touch

After a hard day of crime-fighting, you may wish to have a massage to calm those aching muscles, indulge in some meaningful interaction and promote functional communication. As you massage your hero, be sure to 'listen' to their body cues; try stopping or slowing your rubs to make them 'ask' for more, which is a great way of promoting communication. If appropriate, as you massage, be sure to chat about the amazing adventure they've just been on. What was the best bit? What didn't they like? What is their secret identity?

All senses

When the story has finished, your heroes can go back and choose a preferred activity to revisit. If you've been smart with your choice of props, you may be able to squeeze some extra work out of your superheroes!

DISCOVERY, CREATIVE AND EXPLORATION ACTIVITIES

There are many activities that can be differentiated to explore all things superhero!

Physical challenges and games can empower our superheroes! You can even put these on adapted dice or a randomizer switch. These activities can include:

- 'running' like the Flash

- throwing a frisbee like Captain America or a hammer like Thor

- flying like Superman or Wonder Woman (through creative play, jumping, on a floor surfer or trolley, in a hoist or as part of rebound therapy)

- knocking down bricks like the Hulk

- using a fan linked to a switch to blow down paper villains.

Cosplay is great fun and excellent for promoting play skills and dressing skills and boosting self-esteem. If the story is being told in an environment with many superheroes, try holding a cosplay parade, or competition, where everyone can celebrate the glorious diversity and positivity of all!

Research superheroes through various media, including sequential comic strips. Comics often mirror the sequential nature of symbolized communication which many of our superheroes use and are a fantastic gateway into formal reading. If your heroes are working on mark-making skills, they can create their own comic books – anything from a rip-roaring adventure story to instructions for making a cup of tea or what happens when you visit a dentist.

Design a superhero! Use various mark-making or collage techniques to create your own superhero or superhero costume. You can explore the origins of your superhero, discover what their special powers are and who their nemesis is! This can then be turned into artwork, sequential art, creative writing or even a film.

Make your own super serums! Find interesting bottles and other vessels to make visually stimulating super serums. Add glitter, food colouring or gel, sequins and other items of interest to make a stimulating fidget toy. Alternatively, look up some mocktail recipes to make a range of tasty serums for your heroes to try!

What is super about each other? Find ways to display and discuss the strengths of different people in your group and to celebrate the diversity of peers and friends.

Create a photo booth that looks like a comic panel, Dr Plankenstein's laboratory or a Manhattan-esque skyline. Invite your superheroes to pose in front of it, creating the best comic cover or superhero stance. Use a switch-adapted camera or tablet to allow your superheroes to be in charge of taking photographs of their peers.

Create a story walk – in your setting, you may wish to set up a series of stations that replicate various parts of the story which your learners will tackle sequentially. This can lead them from one area to another and can be useful for those who find transitions difficult.

Try the coloured capes experiment. Have various different coloured capes and invite your superheroes to try them on before completing a timed task or race. Which colour cape makes them go the fastest? Who is in charge of the stopwatch? Who presses the switch to start the race? Can your superheroes order who came first to last, or which activity was quickest?

Exploring good and bad – often the crux of superhero lore is the relationship between good and evil. Try exploring the attributes of being good and strategies to help you regulate when feeling not so virtuous.

You, Me and The Stars
Written up by Katherine Cavill

This story, authored by the students of National Star College, is pure magic. Witnessing its creation was one of the best days of my life. People with profound and multiple learning disabilities have been the consumers of sensory stories since the 1970s, but presumed always to be 'too disabled' to become the creators. However, there is no such thing as 'too disabled' when it comes to the human capacity to be creative. People are, by their very nature, creative, and all disability serves to do is hide that creativity, or impose barriers to our witnessing it. Disability may hamper creativity but it does not impair it, and if we meet the challenge of witnessing it creatively we can find ways to remove those barriers, peek around the obstacles imposed and when we do that...the reward is extraordinary!

When I first shared this story, I ended it by shooting hundreds and thousands of gold stars over the crowd in front of me. People carried those stars away with them, keeping the memory, taking the magic with them. In placing it in this book, I hope to propel those stars even further. Take this story. Tell this story. Follow the stars. Spread the magic of sensory stories!

It's early, time to stretch my limbs and head out to the fields to sew the seeds.
Work is dirty, and hard: Pass more seeds and turn the soil: pass more seeds and turn the soil.
At last a chance to relax tired limbs on the grass.
The sweetness of my tea revives my senses...
...and everything is red.
...
'Where shoes?'
'When the moon comes out do you sleep or do you dance?'

> 'Can you touch the stars?'
> 'Can you see the moon, it is spinning around?'
> 'It's just you, me and the stars.'

INTRODUCTION

This is a romantic story of two people catching each other's eye during the harvest, stealing away to dance together, before ending their day lying gazing up at the stars at the beginning of a love that will last forever.

Authoring

The sequence of the story was created from impressions of the shared expression and creative experience of the authorial team. The second half of the story is composed from words spoken by authors during the writing experience.

   The writing of the story is very much not the authorship of the story. The writing process was the process of trying to articulate what had been witnessed and felt, in terms of atmosphere, events, themes, particular turning points, and so on.

   What we witnessed, what we felt, during the authorship process was created by every single person interacting and exploring the sensations available to them (both those planned prior to the event and ones they drew spontaneously into the experience themselves); consequently, this story is authored by everyone who came through the room.

> It's early, time to stretch my limbs and head out to the fields to sew the seeds.

Hear birdsong. Stretch limbs.

(The authorship began with birdsong, and with all the groups there seemed to be an awakening as awareness of the room and its experiences heightened, yawning was common as people relaxed into the space and began to embrace the experiences on offer.)

> Work is dirty, and hard: Pass more seeds and turn the soil: pass more seeds
> and turn the soil

Pass the seeds in a rhythmic way, and as you pass the seeds chant in a tired way the refrain of 'pass more seeds and turn the soil'.

(During the authorship, a lot of seeds were planted but there was also a sense of some aspects of the work being hard or unpleasant as the soil was often pushed away, or grass rejected. 'Pass more seeds' was expressed by several authors during a very industrious poppy planting session.)

At last a chance to relax tired limbs on the grass.

Rub your limbs to relax them and enjoy the feel of the grass against your skin and its fragrance all around you.

(In all the authoring groups, as the explorations unfolded, a group would gather with the grass or the bamboo fronds for a relaxed time. Often this started peacefully and ended mischievously.)

The sweetness of my tea revives my senses...

Taste (or smell) the honey.

(For many authors, the taste of honey produced smiles and was the moment when the work of exploring the resources turned into the potential for fun. Several authors became willing to engage with resources previously rejected after tasting the honey. Authors reached out to ask for more.)

...and everything is red.

Look through red cellophane to see the world rose tinted.

('Everything is red' was spoken by an author during the authorship process and seemed to reflect the growing flirtatious feel within the room. In being reminded of how as we fall in love, we find that the world takes on a rosy hue.)

Use the bamboo fronds to reach to another person. Shimmy them, rustle them and peek out from behind them.

(This section of the story is without a spoken line, and the flirtatious feel in the room was very tentative; we witnessed lots of sideways glances, stolen looks, glimpses and gentle giggles. In one group, the waving of bamboo fronds drew more and more people in, connecting one to another in a playful way, and out of this sprang hugs, kissing sounds, dancing and hand-holding.)

'Where shoes?'

Dance to the song 'Barefootin'.

(All the authoring groups passed from a phase of getting used to the environment, into a calm exploration that became connective and mischievous: flirtatious. As we tracked this progression onto the story told here, in the words we recognized that in the story two people who had been working side by side had, by this point, noticed each other and begun a more significant connection. There needed to be a point that marked the crossing of that divide, the first gesture of romance that turns friends into something more. In one session, the phrase 'Where shoes?' was declared loudly and clearly and led to spontaneous dancing to this song, which we had not planned on using during the session at all. In the story, the two tired workers, now rested and with energy from the sweet honey, kick off their shoes to dance barefoot in the field among the tall grasses/bamboo.)

At the end of the dancing, breathe in heavy satisfied sighs, akin to the type of deep ssshhh one would use to calm a baby.

(In one authoring session, an author who had previously opted out was enticed to join in by the playfulness of the bamboo frond flirting and as people wafted the bamboo and tickled one another with it he joined in with long slow shhh noises, which in turn calmed the rest of the group.)

> 'When the moon comes out do you sleep or do you dance?'
> 'Can you touch the stars?'
> 'Can you see the moon, it is spinning around?'

Listen to 'Stars of the Lid – The Daughters of Quiet Minds.'
    See the stars twinkling around you (star fairy lights). Intersperse the sentences for this section of the story periodically over the music, allowing a generous pause between each one for reflection.

(The sentences for this part of the story are now the idle musings of two people lying together looking up at the night sky. In the 'Can you see the moon' one we hear one person gently trying to impress another with their knowledge of the night sky. In 'do you sleep or do you dance' there is possibly an invitation to carry on the enjoyment of the day after a point where sleeping would usually be expected. All three sentences were spoken during the authorship process, two by authors and one by two facilitators who asked a group of authors as they were lying under the stars, 'When the moon comes out, do you sleep?' with the second facilitator adding, 'Or do you dance?' At this point the authors clearly stated their inclination by sitting bolt upright.)

'It's just you, me and the stars.'

Shoot star cannons – or shower with golden stars.

(Throughout the connections we made in the authorship sessions – with people reaching out to one another, people unresponsive or unwilling to join in being lured into the mischievousness, one author beginning shy and ending up dancing, another embracing a peer spontaneously in a seeming act of gratitude for the beauty of the moment just shared – everyone in the writing group had a story to tell of a moment they had shared, and the one we selected to end the story was chosen for how well it summarized them all and how confidently it was asserted. After a prolonged period of interaction, this particular author lay down below the star canopy, positioning their face close to the facilitator's, and looked intently into their eyes. As their gaze was returned, they indicated with clear bold gestures the sentence above: 'It's just you, me and the stars.' In our story, this is the end of the tentativeness of the blossoming romance, the connection has been decided and committed to and will last as long as the stars shine and the moon turns.)

ACTIVITIES TO EXPLORE ALONGSIDE THE THEME OF THE STORY

'Pass the seeds and turn the soil'

This is an opportunity for students to pass and stir a mixture of ingredients, such as seeds, spices, flowers, soil, tea leaves, in bowls or trays. Time can be spent choosing and exploring the ingredients, listening to the sounds as they are stirred and scattered into the bowl, exploring movement as they turn and hold the ingredients and equipment, and taking the opportunity to smell and touch the ingredients with their hands or even feet! Participants could begin to pass the ingredients to each other down guttering pipes into each other's bowls, supporting the concept of awareness of 'you and me'.

This could lead on to making seed bombs with the ingredients.

'When the moon comes out do you sleep or do you dance?'

'Can you touch the stars?'
'Can you see the moon, it is spinning around?'
'You, me and the stars.'

Music from the story can be used throughout the session to link story and activity. Create a dark, quiet space with a mixture of lights, torches, lamps and fairy star lights to bring light to the dark room to star gaze! Massage (story massage or hand massages) can be used to support the theme of connection and belonging as a group or on a one-to-one basis. Mirrors can be used to explore reflection of lights, self and others around us through 'catching each other's gaze' through eye contact, facial expressions, vocalizations and verbalizations, intensive interaction and movement.

'At last a chance to relax tired limbs on the grass'
'...and everything is red.'

Explore the colours green, red and darkness and light. This could be created through small black storage boxes with disco lights inside where the colours can be controlled/changed/latch box activated, or fairy lights attached inside to explore light and dark/stars and day.

Create a star/light box with two boxes, with lights/stars on the bottom layer and the second box placed inside this with sand in. As the sand is moved it releases the light from the box below.

Sensory trays that are colour coordinated provide opportunities to explore items from the story such as shoes, cellophane, honey/soil in zip bags creating an array of tactile experiences.

Try painting with these colours and using resources from the story as paint brushes – for example, leaves, bamboo, grass.

'It's early, time to stretch my limbs and head out to the fields to sow the seeds.'

This could open up opportunities to explore movement and music inside and outside. Tai Chi or people's personalized physio stretches could be used to think about stretching 'my limbs'. Music from the story could be played during this activity to create a link between activity and story. People could choose musical instruments for each other to again support the 'you and me' and create opportunities for people to conduct the music (call and response) – my turn, your turn.

Plant seeds and watch them grow in smaller pots, or plant larger trays of grass and wildflower seeds to then explore with feet and hands, creating the opportunity of feeling grass between our toes. Make seed bombs and plants to add to a sensory garden area, which could be used as a storytelling area.

Explore the history of music from around the world such as folk music, harvest songs, love songs, traditional farming songs. Look into creating a call and response song to sing as a group while working in the classroom or while exploring outside areas on walks.

Create a dance alongside the events in the story, exploring light and dark, love and connections, passing and turning, small and growing, fast and slow, through movement and music.

Paul Tarling, Enrichment and Community Engagement Co-ordinator at National Star College, reflected on the feedback that was collected after the authoring. Here are two quotes that gave a wonderful overview of such a remarkable experience:

> What I really loved was being able to see how much students from a different pathway both enjoyed it and were able to engage with it. They engaged in a different way – they asked questions, they explored resources in a deeper way and they talked to each other about their experiences. It was lovely – I was a little bit worried about extending the sensory story to 'more able' learners as I thought it might be too 'low' for them, but I needn't have worried! (Tutor)

> A lemony smell, stroking the foliage separately, then together. A steady caress, eyes wandering, wandering, and then eye contact – fixed. A moment of stillness then broad beaming smiles. Then, rhythmic scrunching, clapping, tapping, passing the plastic. My turn, your turn, my turn, your turn. Faster, faster, slow down stop – and repeat. Finished now. I want to play with someone else. Goodbye, for now. Moonbeam lights the way through a mysterious glade. Hypnotized by the warm glow. A rumble of thunder then I must go... (A facilitator new to sensory storytelling – first observing the workshop and then slowly being encouraged in to the storytelling by our co-authors)

ENDNOTE FROM THE AUTHOR

Thank you for reading my book, I hope it takes you and those you love on a great many sensory adventures together. You will find me online, come and tell me about them!

At the start of this book I thanked the backers of the original sensory story project – the 129 people who believed in me before I was the author of any story or any book. I want to end this second edition of this book with another enormous thank you to them. So many sensory adventures have been had as a result of that first project and I feel as though there are many more to come! Thank you all for being a part of it.

References

Ayer, S. (1998) 'Use of multi-sensory rooms for children with profound and multiple learning disabilities.' *Journal of Learning Disabilities for Nursing, Health and Social Care*, 2(2), 89–97.

Boucher, J. and Bowler, D. (2011) *Memory in Autism: Theory and Evidence*. Cambridge: Cambridge University Press.

ten Brug, A., van der Putten, A., Penne, A., Maes, B. and Vlaskamp, C. (2012) 'Multi-sensory storytelling for persons with profound intellectual and multiple disabilities: An analysis of the development, content and application in practice.' *Journal of Applied Research in Intellectual Disabilities*, 25, 350–359. Available at http://onlinelibrary.wiley.com/doi/10.1111/j.1468-3148.2011.00671.x, accessed 30 July 2014.

Bruner, J.S. (1959) 'The cognitive consequences of early sensory deprivation.' *Psychosomatic Medicine*, 21(2), 89–95.

Doukas, T., Fergusson, A., Fullerton, M. and Grace, J. (2017) *Supporting People with Profound and Multiple Learning Disabilities: Core & Essential Service Standards*. Available at www.pmldlink.org.uk/wp-content/uploads/2017/11/Standards-PMLD-h-web.pdf, accessed 30 May 2021.

Draper, S. (2019) 'How many senses do humans have?' Available at www.psy.gla.ac.uk/~steve/best/senses.html, accessed 16 May 2021.

Dunn, W. (1997) 'The impact of sensory processing abilities on the daily lives of young children and their families: A conceptual model.' *Infants and Young Children*, 9(4), 23–35.

Dunn, W. (2007) 'Supporting children to participate successfully in everyday life by using sensory processing knowledge.' *Infants and Young Children*, 20(2), 84–101. Available at http://depts.washington.edu/isei/iyc/20.2_dunn.pdf, accessed 30 July 2014.

Empson, J. (2012) *Rabbityness*. Swindon: Child's Play (International).

Fairhurst, M. (2014) 'Not 5 but 33 senses.' Arts & Humanities Research Council. Available at www.sciculture.ac.uk/2014/06/12/not-5-but-33-senses, accessed 16 May 2021.

Fuller, C. (1999a) 'Fiction for adults with profound learning difficulties.' *PMLD Link*, 12(1), 11–13.

Fuller, C. (1999b) 'Bag books tactile stories.' *The SLD Experience*, 23, 20–21.

Gabbard, C. and Rodrigues, L. (2007) 'Optimizing early brain and motor development through movement.' *Early Childhood News*. Available at http://docplayer.net/25393454-Optimizing-early-brain-and-motor-development-through-movement-by-carl-gabbard-ed-d-and-luis-rodrigues.html, accessed 1 April 2022.

Glenn, S. (1987) 'Interactive Approaches to Working with Children with Profound and Multiple Learning Difficulties.' In B. Smith (ed.), *Interactive Approaches to the Education of Children with Severe Learning Difficulties*. Birmingham: Westhill College.

Grace, J. (2016) *When You Were Gone*. The Sensory Projects. Available at www.thesensoryprojects.co.uk/sensory-stories, accessed 1 April 2022.

Grace, J. (2018a) *Sharing Sensory Stories and Conversations with People with Dementia*. London: Jessica Kingsley Publishers.

Grace, J. (2018b) *Sensory-Being for Sensory Beings*. London: Routledge.

Grace, J. (2018c) *Ernest and I*. Hyde: LDA Resources.

Grace, J. (2019) 'Sensory stories – self-expression through sensory experience.' *SEN Leader*, 26, 15–16.

Grace, J. and Robinson, L. (2017) 'Co-authoring sensory stories with individuals with PMLD.' *PMLD Link*, 29(3), 88, 28–31. Available at www.pmldlink.org.uk/wp-content/uploads/2018/01/PMLD-Link-Issue-88.pdf, accessed 1 April 2022.

Grace, J. and Silva, A. (2017) 'Refining the guidance for sensory storytelling with individuals with PMLD: A move towards improved research and practice.' *PMLD Link*, 29(3), 88, 11–14.

Gray, G. and Chasey, C. (2006) 'SMILE: A new service development for people with profound and multiple learning disabilities.' *PMLD Link*, 18, 3(55), 27–31.

Grove, N. (2012) *Using Storytelling to Support Children and Adults with Special Needs: Transforming Lives through Telling Tales*. London: Routledge.

Grove, N. and Park, K. (1996) *Odyssey Now*. London: Jessica Kingsley Publishers.

Grove, N and Park, K. (2001) *Social Cognition through Drama and Literature for People with Learning Disabilities*. London: Jessica Kingsley Publishers.

Grove, N. (2020) https://www.survivingthroughstory.com and https://www.openstorytellers.org.uk

Hayes, S., McGuire, B., O'Neill, M., Oliver, C. and Morrison, T. (2011) 'Low mood and challenging behaviour in people with severe and profound intellectual disabilities.' *Journal of Intellectual Disability Research*, 55(2), 182–189. Available at http://onlinelibrary.wiley.com/doi/10.1111/j.1365-2788.2010.01355.x, accessed 30 July 2014.

Helton, S. (2017) *A Special Kind of Grief*. London: Jessica Kingsley Publishers.

Jarrold, C., Nadel, L. and Vicari, S. (2008) 'Memory and neuropsychology in Down syndrome.' *Downs Syndrome Education Online*. Available at www.down-syndrome.org/reviews/2068, accessed 20 June 2014.

Lacey, P. (2006) 'Inclusive literacy.' *PMLD Link: Changing Perspectives*, 18, 3(55), 11–13.

Lacey, P. (2009) 'Developing the thinking of people with profound and multiple learning disabilities.' *PMLD Link: Sharing Perspectives*, 21(63), 15–20.

Lambe, L. *et al.* (2014) 'The use of a personalised multi-sensory story to prepare a young man with profound intellectual disabilities and autism for oral health care: A case study.' *Journal of Disability and Oral Health*, 15(4), 154–158.

Leighton, R., Oddy, C. and Grace, J. (2016) 'Using sensory stories with individuals with dementia.' *Journal of Dementia Care*, 24(4), 28–31. And in the *Australian Journal of Dementia Care*. Available at https://journalofdementiacare.com/using-sensory-stories-with-individuals-with-dementia, accessed 30 May 2021.

Longhorn, F. (1988) *A Sensory Curriculum for Very Special People: A Practical Approach to Curriculum Planning*. London: Souvenir Press.

Macpherson, F. (2011) *The Senses: Classic and Contemporary Philosophical Readings*. Oxford: Oxford University Press. Available at www.gla.ac.uk/media/Media_176732_smxx.pdf, accessed 16 May 2021.

Ockenden, J. (2006) 'The development of a culture of engagement in a service supporting adults with profound and multiple learning disabilities.' *PMLD Link: Changing Perspectives*, 18, 3(55), 3–8.

Owen, J.P., Elysa J., Marco, E.J., Desai, S. *et al.* (2013) 'Abnormal white matter microstructure in children with sensory processing disorders.' *NeuroImage: Clinical*, 2, 844–853. Available at www.sciencedirect.com/science/article/pii/S2213158213000776, accessed 30 July 2014.

Park, K. (2004) 'Interactive storytelling: From the Book of Genesis.' *British Journal of Special Education*, 31(1), 16–23.

Piaget J. (1952) *The Origins of Intelligence in Children*. M. Cook, translator. New York, International Universities Press.

Pollitt, K. (1991) 'Hers; The Smurfette Principle.' *The New York Times*. Available at www.nytimes.com/1991/04/07/magazine/hers-the-smurfette-principle.html, accessed 30 July 2014.

Preece, D. and Zhao, Y. (2015) 'Multi-sensory storytelling in special school settings.' *British Journal of Special Education*, 42(4), 429–443.

Swanson, L H. (1993) 'Working memory in learning disability subgroups.' *Journal of Experimental Child Psychology*, 56(1), 87–114.

Vlaskamp, C. and Cuppen-Fonteine, H. (2007) 'Reliability of assessing the sensory perception of children with profound intellectual and multiple disabilities: A case study.' *Child: Care, Health and Development*, 33(5), 547–551.

Vlaskamp, C., Hiemstra, S.J. and Wiersma, L.A. (2007) 'Becoming aware of what you know or need to know: Gathering client and context characteristics in day services for persons with profound intellectual and multiple disabilities.' *Journal of Policy and Practice in Intellectual Disabilities*, 4(2), 97–103.

Watson, M. (2002) *Developing Literacy Skills through Multi-sensory Story-telling in Children and Young Adults with Profound and Multiple Learning Disabilities*. Dundee: University of Dundee.

Young, H. and Lambe, L. (2011) 'Multi-sensory story telling for people with profound and multiple learning disabilities.' *PMLD Link*, 23, 1(68), 29–31.

Young, H., Lambe, L., Fenwick, M. and Hogg, J. (2011) 'Multi-sensory storytelling as an aid to assisting people with profound intellectual disabilities to cope with sensitive issues: A multiple research methods analysis of engagement and outcomes.' *European Journal of Special Needs Education*, 26(2), 127–142.

Further Reading

Autistic UK CIC (2020) *Identity-first Language*. Autistic UK CIC. Available at https://autisticuk. org/resources/identity-first-language, accessed 2 July 2020.

Bonnello, C. (2018) *11,521 People Answered this Autism Survey. Warning: The Results May Challenge You*. Autistic Not Weird. Available at https://autisticnotweird.com/2018survey, accessed 2 July 2020.

Brown, L. (2011a) *Identity-first Language*. ASAN. Available at https://autisticadvocacy.org/aboutasan/identity-first-language, accessed 2 July 2020.

Brown, L. (2011b) *Identity and Hypocrisy: A Second Argument against Person-first Language*. Autistic Hoya. Available at www.autistichoya.com/2011language, accessed 2 July 2020.

Fuller, C. (2012) 'Multi-Sensory Stories in Story-Packs.' In N. Grove (ed.), *Using Storytelling to Support Children and Adults with Special Needs: Transforming Lives through Telling Tales*. London: Routledge.

Gernsbacher, M.A. (2017) 'Editorial perspective: The use of person-first language in scholarly writing may accentuate stigma.' *Journal of Child Psychology and Psychiatry, and Allied Disciplines*, 58(7), 859–861. https://doi.org/10.1111/jcpp.12706.

Identity-First Autistic (n.d.) *Autistic Is Not a Dirty Word*. Available at www.identityfirstautistic. org, accessed 2 July 2020.

Jess at Diary of a Mom (2012) *Person First: An Evolution in Thinking*. Thinking Person's Guide to Autism. Available at www.thinkingautismguide.com/2012/07/person-first-evolution-in-thinking.html, accessed 2 July 2020.

Longhorn, F. (1988) *A Sensory Curriculum for Very Special People*. London: Souvenir Press. (Available for free along with lots of other sensory resources from: https://sites.google. com/view/flolonghornsensorybooksfreedow/home).

Longhorn, F. (2011) 'A short history of shout, glow, jump, taste, smell, touch and wobble: Multi-sensory education (part 2).' *PMLD Link*, 23, 1(68), 29–31.

McCann, L. (2017) *Why I Am Changing My Language about Autism*. Reach Out ASC. Available at www.reachoutasc.com/blog/why-i-m-changing-my-language-about-autism-1, accessed 2 July 2020.

Milton, D. (2017) 'Difference Versus Disability: Implications of Characterisation of Autism for Education and Support.' In R. Jordan (ed.), *The Sage Handbook of Autism and Education*. London: Sage.

Olusoga, D. (2017) *Black and British: A Forgotten History*. London: Picador.

PAMIS (2002) *Real Lives: Real Stories – Summary of Results Developing Literacy Skills through Multi-sensory Story-telling in Children and Young People with Profound and Multiple Learning Disabilities* [Brochure].

Rose, K. (2017) *I Do Not HAVE Autism*. The Autistic Advocate. Available at https://theautisticadvocate.com/ 2017/10/i-do-not-have-autism, accessed 2 July 2020.

Simmons, B. (2011) 'The "profound and multiple learning disabilities ambiguity": Articulating the lifeworlds of children with profound and multiple learning difficulties.' Paper presented at: the Nordic Network on Disability Research (NNDR) 11th Annual Conference, Reykjavik, Iceland (28 May 2011).

Simmons, B. and Bayliss, P. (2007) 'The role of special education for children with profound and multiple learning difficulties: Is segregation always best?' *British Journal of Special Education*, 34(1), 19–24.

Sinclair, J. (1999) 'Why I dislike "person first" language.' Available at https://autisticuk.org/wp-content/uploads/2016/05/AUTISTIC-UK-KEY-TEXTS-1-WHY-I-DISLIKE-PERSON-FIRST-LANGUAGE.pdf, accessed 2 July 2020.

Sparrow, M. (2017) 'Labels are valuable tools.' Thinking Person's Guide to Autism. Available at www.thinkingautismguide.com/2017/11/labels-are-valuabletools.html, accessed 2 July 2020.

Taylor, J. (2006) 'Using multi-sensory stories to develop literacy skills and to teach sensitive topics.' *PMLD Link: Changing Perspectives*, 18, 3(55), 14–16.

Thurman, S. (2011) 'Is communication a human right for people with profound and multiple learning disabilities?' *PMLD Link: Speaking Up, Being Heard* 23, 1(68), 10–15.

Index

Bold entries refer to organisations.

achievement celebration 76, 184
anxiety 23–24, 69–72, 112
assessment 76–77
autism/autistic 22, 45, 51, 59–61 164

Bag Books 9, 13, 32
Bamboozle 9
Benjamin, Gwendolen 29–30, 32, 141
bereavement 31
bookending 74–75

Cavill, K 186
celebrate 58, 76, 174, 176, 178, 185
Changing Places 35
Circus Starr 35, 71
co-active movement 167, 170,
co-authoring sensory stories 36, 186, 192
cognitive capacity 59–60
cognitive development 19, 21
communication difficulties 63, 69
communication switches 43–43,
     159, 176, 183–186
compression wear 24
concentration 61
confidence 30, 33, 49–50, 56, 63, 176
consistency 31, 39–42, 47–48, 53, 64–65, 137
coping strategies 30, 56–57, 59–60,
*Core and Essential Service Standards for
     Supporting People with Profound and
     Multiple Learning Disabilities* 47
creative writing 72

dementia 26, 35

distillation of stories 73

eating 53, 57–58, 112–113, 118, 122, 124–125
Empson, J. *Rabbityness,* 30
engagement 22–23, 47, 59, 62,
     69, 76–78, 81, 174, 192
epilepsy 47–49
Ernest and I 29

fear 23, 30, 113
fiddle toys 24, 185
fidgeting 23, 61
fight or flight 23, 181
fine motor 156
Frozen Light 34

grief 31
Grove, N 9, 13, 65, 162, 164

Head2Head 9
Heligan Gardens 34
Helton, S 31
Hirstwood, R 20

identity 29, 83, 184,
information overload 59–60
interaction 13, 42, 54–55, 69,
     101, 180–181, 184, 190

kayaking 35
Kensington Palace 35, 71–72
Kickstarter 9, 33

King Edward Mine 35

literacy 14, 31–32, 63
London Transport Museum 35

Makaton 168
massage 157, 179, 184, 191
memory 31, 48, 59, 64, 91, 97, 106, 181, 186
mental health 65, 176
Mutwa, C 164

National Star College 186, 192
Navin, V 153
neurodivergent 45, 51, 59, 65
neurological thresholds 52, 54, 55, 65
Ntanzi, M 164–165

Oily Cart 9
Open Story Tellers Project 65, 162
overwhelm 45, 51–54, 57, 60,
        65, 69, 97, 119, 122

PAMIS (Promoting A More
        Inclusive Society) 13, 32, 47
Parallel Lifestyle 35
passivity 22, 52, 120
PECS (Picture Exchange
        Communication System) 162
physical impairments 21
PMLD link 31, 36
preferences 26, 39–40, 45, 47–48,
        55, 57, 76, 78, 120
proprioception 19, 23, 27, 117, 131, 134–135,
        137, 156, 158, 167, 169–171, 178–184
Purple Goat 12

reactions 40, 52, 56–57, 77–78,
        121, 170, 178, 181

recording 56–57, 77–78
repetition 31, 39, 42, 65, 75, 162
Rhyming Multisensory Stories 153

self-harm 22, 52
sensory accessibility 35, 71
sensory barriers 154
Sensory-being for Sensory Beings 27
sensory capacity 62
sensory impairment 47
sensory processing disorder/
        differences 51–57, 59–60
Sensory Story Project 14, 32–33
sensory systems (including
        subconscious senses) 22, 54
*Sharing Sensory Stories and Conversations
        with People with Dementia* 26, 35
Sibley, M 12
sign language, key signs 168, 183
social model of disability 11, 165
super sensory race 35
Surviving Through Story 65, 162

Tarling, P 192
teaching assistants 14, 43
The Birth of a Star 32, 60, 64
The Special Storyteller 174–175

University of Exeter 33, 35

vestibular 23, 27, 117, 133, 135, 156, 158, 180
vibration 120, 130–140, 166
vocalization 44, 70, 78, 97, 191

wellbeing 176, 184
Wells, P 9, 32, 174, 175

Zulu 162, 165–166, 168, 173–174